Basketball's Offensive Sets

Winning Half-Court Strategy

—— Tom Reiter ——

mp
MASTERS PRESS

NTC/Contemporary Publishing Group

Library of Congress Cataloging-in-Publication Data

Basketball's offensive sets : winning half-court strategy / Tom Reiter.
   p.   cm.
   ISBN 1-57028-040-1
    1. Basketball—Offense.   2. Half-court basketball.   I. Title.
GV889.R425   1995
796.323′2—dc20   95-37326
                                     CIP

Cover design by Nick Panos
Cover photograph copyright © 1998 Todd Warshaw/Allsport USA
Edited by Kim Heusel
Text layout by Holly Kondras
Diagram reproduction by Phil Velikan and Kelli Ternet

Published by Masters Press
A division of NTC/Contemporary Publishing Group, Inc.
4255 West Touhy Avenue, Lincolnwood (Chicago), Illinois 60646-1975 U.S.A.
Copyright © 1995 by Tom Reiter
Printed in the United States of America
International Standard Book Number: 1-57028-040-1
      02 03 04 BP 19 18 17 16 15 14 13 12 11 10 9 8 7

Acknowledgments

All books are cooperative efforts. Writers are always dependent upon others for their ideas and critiques. I want to thank the many coaches who have made suggestions regarding this book, Coach Gene Keady and his fine staff, especially his fine assistant coach, Bruce Weber, for their advice and insights.

I am grateful to Kim Heusel for all his help in editing and smoothing of the rough edges and Kathy O'Brien for her hard work in preparation of the manuscript.

I also want to acknowledge Masters Press and Tom Bast in particular for their patience and encouragement.

I want to thank my lovely wife, Stacie Hitt, for her support and advice in putting this project together; my sons, Matt and Dan, for providing the ubiquitous sound of driveway basketball that has supplied the accompaniment for the writing of so much of this book.

Finally, I want to express my appreciation to my sons' Parks and Rec coaches, who allowed me to view the game from the perspective of a fan. It motivated me to get this work out as quickly as possible.

Table of Contents

"A calculated risk is a known risk for the sake of a real gain. A risk for the sake of a risk is a fool's choice."

Bugle Notes
United States Military Academy

Foreword

The original idea for this project was to present a collection of "quick hitters" designed to get a shot after one or two passes, but as the work progressed it grew into the book as it now exists. The additions I made to this volume expand the usefulness of the quick hitters so that they can be used alone or as entry into the passing game. While the continuity sets I have included can be used as quick hitters, they also provide options to coaches whose teams may need more structure. Included are a number of offenses originating out of various alignments: high post, high 1-4, and box set. Using the same alignments for your offense, while also incorporating quick hitter options, creates difficulties for opponents in anticipating plays and discerning tendencies.

The need for quick hitters is most apparent now in basketball for two reasons. Possession time by the offense has been greatly reduced. The tempo of the game has quickened considerably and, even though the offense may have more total possessions in the course of the game, the time per possession has decreased.

The second reason for the need for quick hitters is that defenses now extend further out on the floor in an attempt to force the offense to use more of its valuable time in fighting full-court or three-quarter-court pressure. This forces a smaller window of opportunity in which to decide who shoots the ball and from where on the floor it will be attempted. For these reasons, the coach's responsibility is to have the team organized and prepared to meet these challenges on almost every offensive possession. More often than not this is the difference between victory and defeat.

I hope you will find something in this collection that will be useful to you as you prepare your team for the multitude of situations that present themselves in the course of a game. Those of you familiar with my earlier book, *Basketball Inbound Attack*, will find the format and organization similar. In this collection I have attempted to incorporate more narrative descriptions of the diagrams and add more detail. I think you will find it helpful. Best of luck.

Key to Diagrams

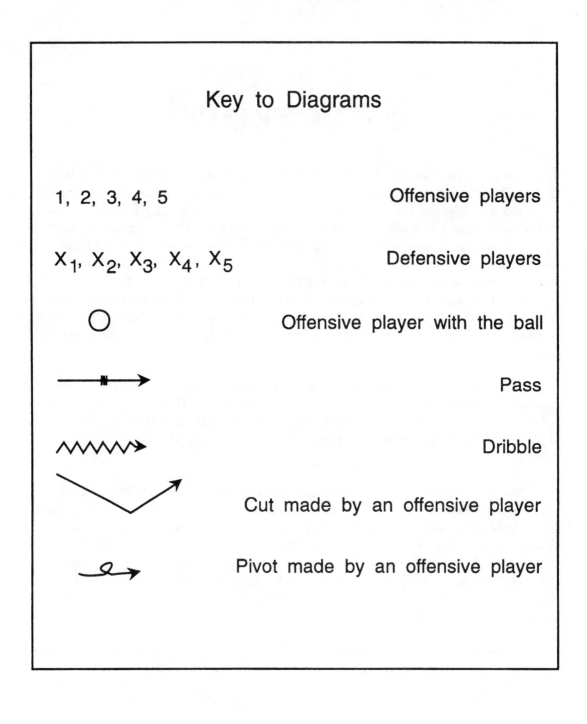

1, 2, 3, 4, 5 — Offensive players

X_1, X_2, X_3, X_4, X_5 — Defensive players

◯ — Offensive player with the ball

— Pass

— Dribble

— Cut made by an offensive player

— Pivot made by an offensive player

The High 1-4

The options out of the high 1-4 set seem almost limitless. It is a good alignment initially because the offense is up off of the baseline and defensive help is weak. This creates backcut possibilities for layups, and cutters also have room as they come off of screens. Also, the ball can be entered to any of the other four players, putting even more pressure on the defense.

A

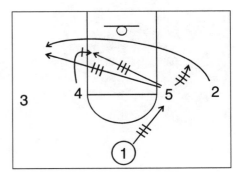

Player No. 1 passes to No. 5 and No. 2 immediately cuts backdoor looking for a layup from No. 5's pass. Player No. 4 drops to the block to screen for No. 2 as he cuts along the baseline. Player No. 5 can pass to No. 2 or to No. 4 who posts up after No. 2 has cut.

B

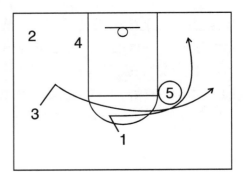

Player No. 1 holds his spot on the point until No. 2 has made his cut. Player No. 1 then sets his defender up with a "V-cut" and cuts off of No. 5 looking for a handoff. The side is cleared out for 1-on-1. Player No. 3 follows No. 1's cut and curls around No. 5, except No. 3 is looking for the jump shot.

C

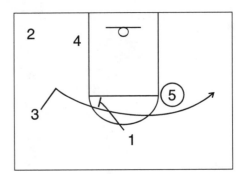

Option: Player No. 1 can screen away for No. 3 as No. 3 cuts around No. 5 instead of having No. 1 occupy the vacated wing.

A

Here No. 1 passes to the wing man, No. 2. Player No. 5 then drops to the ballside block for a post up. Player No. 4 steps up to the circle to screen for No. 1 who cuts hard looking for the lob pass. Player No. 3 stays wide so his defender can't help.

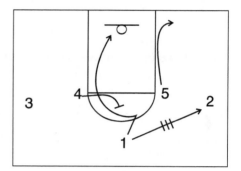

B

After No. 4 screens for No. 1, he steps to the ball to receive the pass. Player No. 1 sets his man up as No. 3 comes down from the weakside wing to screen for No. 1 on the weakside block.

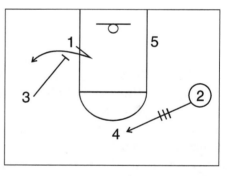

C

After No. 1 receives the pass, No. 3 will look to post up momentarily to get his defender to fight for defensive post position. Player No. 3 then turns to screen for No. 5 (this is a "little on big" screen so most teams will be reluctant to switch this). Player No. 4 then screens for No. 3 who will come to the free-throw line looking for a jump shot.

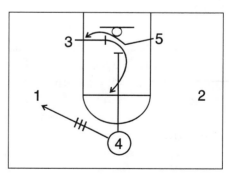

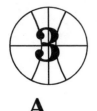

Triangle Game High 1-4

A

Player No. 1 passes to No. 5 at the wing and then makes a corner cut.

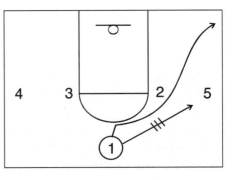

B

Player No. 3 drops to the opposite block as No. 4 comes across the lane to screen for No. 2. Player No. 2 receives the ball from No. 5.

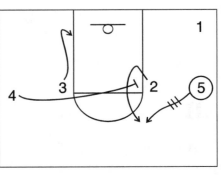

C

Player No. 2 then dribbles toward No. 3's wing. As the ball is being brought to No. 3's side, No. 3 looks to go backdoor for a layup if he is being overplayed. Player No. 5 holds his position until he sees what No. 3 is going to do. Player No. 5 then cuts off of No. 4. Player No. 2 dribbles the ball to the wing.

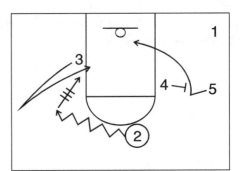

D

As No. 2 dribbles into position to create a passing lane just below the free-throw line extended, No. 3 momentarily posts up on the ballside block. If No. 3 can't receive the pass from No. 2, he turns and screens across the lane for No. 5. This screen may create a mismatch if there is a switch. Player No. 4 then screens down for No. 3 creating a "pick-the-picker" situation. Player No. 1 stays wide on the weak side to eliminate weakside help.

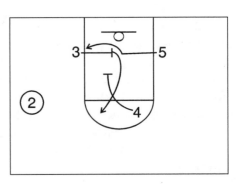

A

Player No. 1 passes to No. 2 and cuts down the middle of the lane. As No. 1 is cutting, No. 4 screens across the lane for No. 3 who dives to the ballside block. Player No. 5 rotates to the top of the circle.

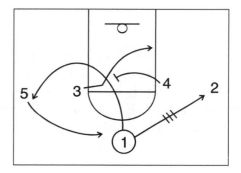

B

If No. 3 does not receive the pass from No. 2 the ball is reversed to No. 5. Player No. 3 backscreens for No. 2 as No. 5 swings the ball to No. 1. Player No. 5 then screens for No. 3 for the jump shot.

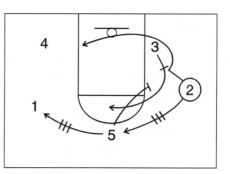

C

Player No. 1 passes the ball to No. 5. Once No. 5 has received the pass, No. 2 cuts hard to the basket for a backdoor layup. As this is taking place, both No. 3 and No. 4 tighten up on the opposite block for a double screen for No. 2. Player No. 1 follows his pass to No. 5 looking for a hand off or return pass because this side is cleared out for No. 1 to be isolated with his defender.

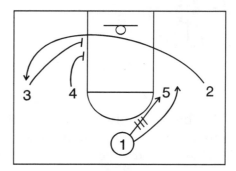

High 1-4 Set

A

Player No. 4 screens on the ball as No. 2 slides to an open area. If No. 2's defender helps on No. 1, No. 2 will get a pass and an uncontested shot. After No. 4 screens on the ball, No. 5 will screen No. 4's defender (pick-the-picker).

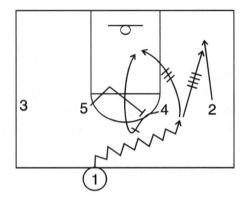

B

Player No. 1 dribbles to No. 2's wing and No. 2 empties out cutting through he lane. Player No. 1 then crosses over with his dribble as No. 5 steps up to screen on No. 1's defender. Both No. 3 and No. 4 screen No. 2's defender for No. 2 to be able to catch the ball for the jump shot.

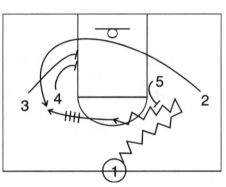

A

This is simply a "penetrate and pitch" situation out of the high 1-4 set. Player No. 2 slides toward the baseline as he sees No. 1 bring the ball to that wing.

Player No. 5 screens across the lane for No. 4, who curls down the middle of the lane looking for a pass from No. 1.

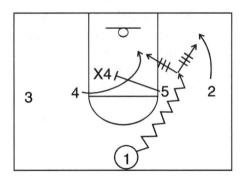

A

Another option out of a high 1-4 set is the "dribble out" option. Player No. 1 dribbles toward No. 3 who curls around No. 4. Player No. 4 sinks a little below the free-throw line along the lane. Players No. 5 and No. 2 stay wide.

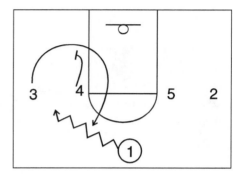

B

Player No. 1 looks to give a quick post feed to No. 4 whose man may try to give momentary help on No. 3's curl. Player No. 1 passes to No. 3 and, as soon as No. 3 catches, No. 5 steps out away from the lane to screen for No. 2 who makes a curl cut into the lane for a jump shot, layup or a pick and roll with No. 5 after No. 2 catches the ball.

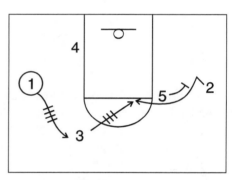

C

After No. 3 has received the pass from No. 1, No. 3 can skip pass to No. 2 and have No. 5 drop to the low post for a two man game. Player No. 4 comes up the lane line to back screen for No. 3. This also eliminates weakside help as No. 5 attempts to gain control of the ballside block.

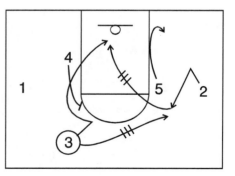

1-4 Set

A

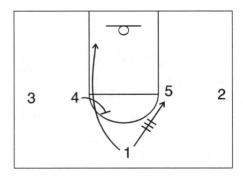

Player No. 1 passes the ball to No. 5 at the high post. Player No. 4 steps up to backscreen for No. 1 who will look for a lob pass or possible layup. If No. 1 doesn't receive the ball, he will hold his spot at the block.

B

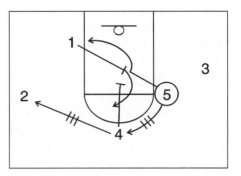

Player No. 5 then reverses the ball to No. 4 who, in turn, passes it to No. 2 on the wing. Player No. 1 then sets a diagonal screen for No. 5 for a layup. Player No. 4 will screen for No. 1 and if No. 1's defender helps on No. 5's cut, No. 1 will have an excellent look at the basket for an open shot.

A

This is a quick hitter for your best shooter out of the 1-4 set. Player No. 1 dribbles away from No. 2 as No. 4 and No. 5 set a double staggered screen for No. 2 who should catch inside the circle. If a 3-point field goal is needed, the angle of screens and the cut toward the ball should be adjusted.

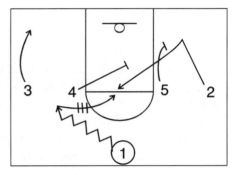

B

When No. 2 catches he looks to score. If he can't get his opening, both No. 4 and No. 5 turn back into the lane and screen again, this time for No. 3 who cuts across the lane. Player No. 2 can also pass to No. 1 for a shot or post feed or No. 2 can go directly inside with a pass.

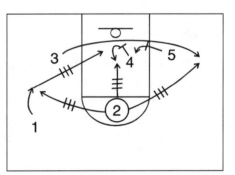

A

If you would rather create a two man game on the weak side with a perimeter player and post man, the same cuts are initially made. Player No. 1 passes to No. 2 and cuts off No. 5. At the same time, No. 3 cuts to the ballside corner underneath No. 1.

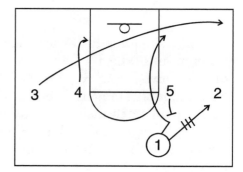

B

Player No. 2 then receives a screen from No. 5. Player No. 1 runs the baseline as No. 4 screens for No. 1 at the block. Player No. 2 can penetrate to the hoop, he can execute the pick and roll with No. 5. Player No. 2 can also pass to No. 1 for a jump shot or, after No. 1 catches the ball, he can look inside to No. 4 for the two-man game.

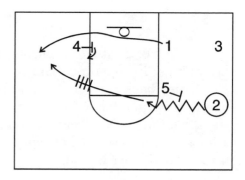

A

Here No. 1 passes to the wing (No. 2), and cuts off of the ballside high post man (No. 5). Player No. 4 drops to the opposite block.

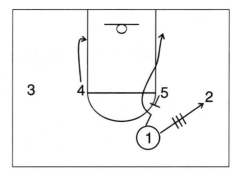

B

After No. 5 has screened for No. 1, No. 5 then steps out and screens on the ball for a pick and roll. As No. 2 dribbles the ball over No. 5's screen, both No. 3 and No. 4 set a double screen for No. 1 who runs the baseline looking for the ball.

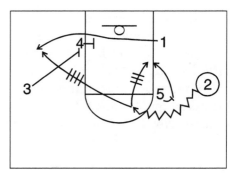

A

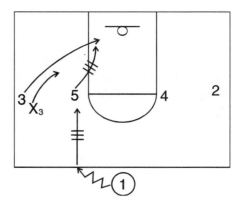

This is a backdoor option out of the 1-4 set. The first option is the guard passing to one of the post players positioned at the corner of the free-throw line. If the wing man on his side is being overplayed (as in diagram A) the wing cuts hard for a layup.

B

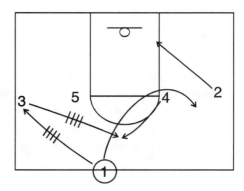

If No. 1 passes to No. 3, the passer loops underneath No. 4 and No. 4 steps to the top of the circle to receive a pass. Player No. 5 turns to No. 3 looking for the ball but stays high. Player No. 2 cuts to the weakside block as No. 3 has the ball. Player No. 4 receives the pass from No. 3.

C

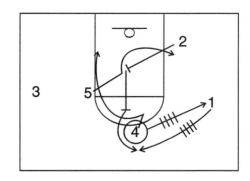

Player No. 4 reverses the ball to No. 1 on the weak side who looks for a possible post up by No. 2. Player No. 2 diagonally up screens for No. 5 who cuts hard to post up or get a layup. Player No. 2 screens again, but this time it is a backscreen for No. 4 for a potential lob pass from No. 1. Player No. 2 then steps to the ball because his man will have to help on the backscreen.

Here No. 1 passes to the wing and receives a high post screen from No. 4.

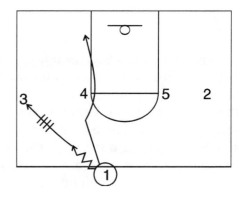

B

The opposite big man steps up and the ball is reversed. As No. 2 is catching the ball, No. 1 backscreens for No. 3 who shuffle cuts to the ballside block looking for a layup. Then both No. 4 and No. 5 screen down for No. 1.

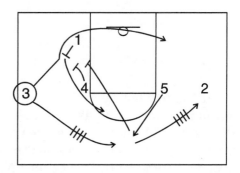

A

This is a very effective option out of the 1-4 set. Here the point man passes to one of the high post men (No. 4) and cuts down the lane. Player No. 1 then turns and screens No. 5 as No. 5 cuts on top of the screen looking for a layup. If the defense switches, there is a mismatch created inside with a guard defending an inside player.

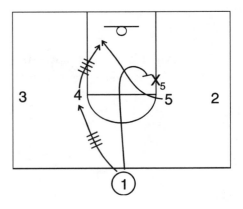

B

If No. 5 is not open, No. 1 steps back out of the lane for a pass from No. 4. Player No. 5 then turns and seals for a high/low pass. If No. 1 catches the ball and is open, he shoots it. Oftentimes No. 1's defender will momentarily help on No. 5's cut to the basket. This gives No. 1 an advantage in getting free for an open look at the hoop.

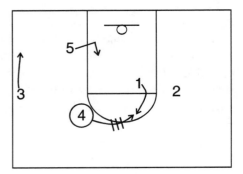

This is a simple option out of the 1-4 to get the ball inside. Player No. 2 screens at the free-throw line for No. 4 who pops out to catch the ball at the wing. After No. 4 receives the pass, No. 2 continues across the lane to screen for No. 5 who dives to the basket off of No. 2's screen.

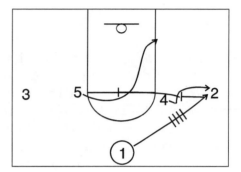

A

This is an excellent option out of the 1-4 set. It is a clear out for a two-man game. This isolation play forces the defense to decide how they will defend a very quick hitting offensive maneuver.

Player No. 1 passes the ball to No. 3 and the wing and cuts to the ballside corner.

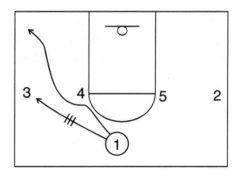

B

Player No. 3 passes the ball to No. 1 in the corner. Player No. 4 then comes out to the screen on the ball as No. 3 cuts across the lane clearing out the side for a two-man game. Player No. 1 and No. 4 run a pick and roll as both No. 2 and No. 5 flare screen for No. 3.

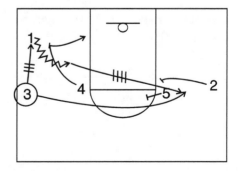

A

This is a lob play out of the 1-4 set. Player No. 1 dribbles toward No. 3's side and he empties out to the other side of the floor. As No. 3 is cutting, No. 5 cuts down the lane line and across to the ballside block. Player No. 2 tightens up on the weakside block to screen for No. 3 as No. 3 cuts through the lane.

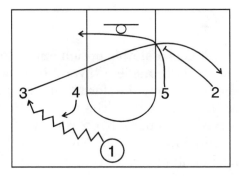

B

Player No. 1 now looks to No. 5 at the low post. Player No. 2 now backscreens for No. 4 for a lob pass to the basket.

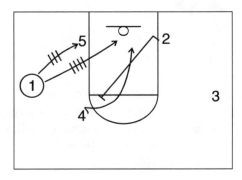

C

Player No. 2 reverses the ball to No. 1. Now No. 3 uses the double screen as he cuts along the baseline for the basketball.

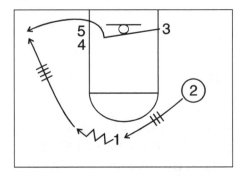

A

This series begins with a "dribble out" option. Player No. 1 dribbles to No. 2's side and No. 2 curls around No. 5. Player No. 3 cuts to the ballside corner.

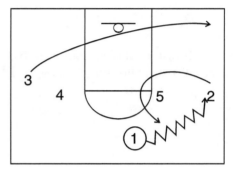

B

Player No. 1 reverses the ball to No. 2 and both No. 5 and No. 1 double screen for No. 3 who cuts hard looking for a jump shot. Player No. 2 also has the option of looking for No. 4 as he posts-up on the other side of the floor at this offense consistently looks for the pass into the low post area.

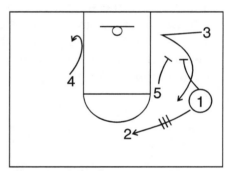

A

Same entry as above as No. 1 dribbles No. 2 from the wing position. Player No. 1 then passes to No. 2.

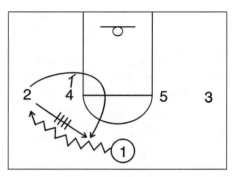

B

After No. 2 catches the ball, both No. 4 and No. 5 double screen on the side the ball was dribbled toward. This creates a clear out for No. 3. Player No. 2 and No. 3 create a two man game as No. 3 posts up his defender.

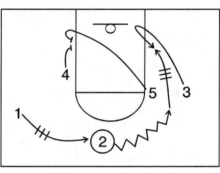

C

This is a "dribble out" option as No. 1 takes the ball to the wing. Player No. 4 screens across the lane for No. 5 who dives to the ballside block looking for the post up. Player No. 4 then screens for No. 2 who cuts up the middle of the lane for a possible jump shot at the top of the circle.

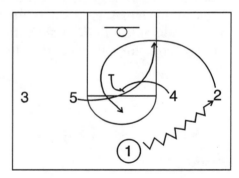

D

Player No. 1 looks into the post or back to the middle of the floor as passing options.

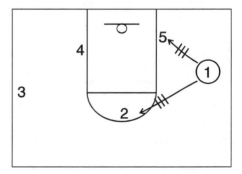

A

This is the same "dribble out" option designed to get No. 1 a jump shot or as a secondary option to get the ball inside. Player No. 1 dribbles No. 2 from the wing. Player No. 3 cuts to the corner.

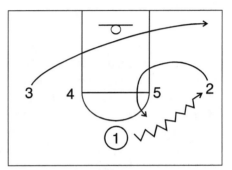

B

Player No. 2 receives the ball at the top of the circle. After No. 1 passes, he cuts to the block. As No. 2 dribbles to No. 4's side, No. 5 steps up for a return pass.

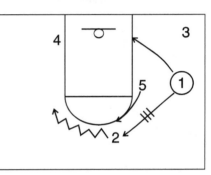

C

Player No. 2 quickly reverse the ball to No. 5 and No. 3 then screens for No. 1 along the baseline. Player No. 5 passes the ball to No. 1.

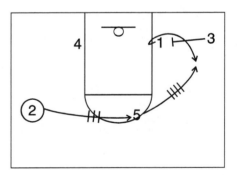

D

If No. 1 catches but does not shoot No. 4 backscreens No. 3's defender as No. 3 curls around the top of the screen. If No. 3's defender doesn't switch the screen, No. 4 steps toward the ball for a post feed from No. 1.

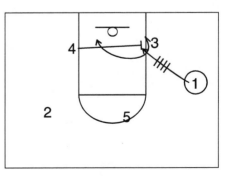

A

Player No. 1 dribbles off No. 5's screen and No. 5 rolls to the basket. No. 4 will screen on No. 5's defender as No. 5 cuts to the hoop. Player No. 2 cuts through the lane and No. 3 screens for him. Player No. 2's cut empties out the side where No. 5 is making his basket cut.

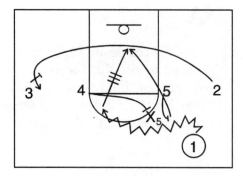

The Box Set

This section contains quick hitters out of the box set. The alignment is very effective for a number of reasons:

- It's virtually impossible for the defense to predict what the offense is prepared to execute because of the multitude of options in its cutting and screening action.

- This alignment puts an unusual amount of pressure on the defense because the ball can be placed in a scoring area after only one pass. It can be accomplished either at the wing or in the low post.

- The set opens up the possibility of forcing the interior defenders to come out onto the floor to defend on the perimeter.

A

Player No. 1 dribbles to the wing and No. 4 cuts hard to receive the pass from No. 1. Player No. 4 then reverses the ball No. 2.

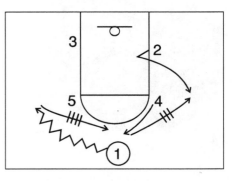

B

Players No. 5 and No. 4 screen down for No. 3. The screeners set staggered screens for No. 3. This provides an opportunity for either of the screeners to roll toward the ballside block if their defenders attempt to help on No. 3's cut.

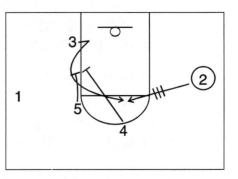

A

Player No. 1 dribbles the ball to the wing as No. 5 goes to screen for No. 3. Player No. 3 receives the ball in the corner as No. 5 continues across the lane to screen again for No. 2. Player No. 5 can turn back toward the ball after he screens No. 2. Player No. 4 looks for the open area along the weak side.

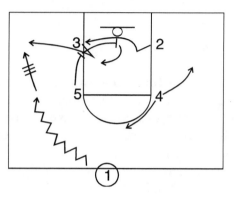

A

This is a lob play out of a box set. Player No. 1 dribbles the ball to the wings as No. 4 screens for No. 3. Player No. 4 continues out to the corner. Player No. 3 receives the ball at the wing. At the same time on the weak side, No. 5 downscreens for No. 2. Instead of accepting No. 5's screens, No. 2 fakes toward the wing but cuts to the ballside block.

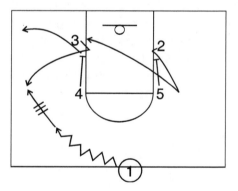

B

Player No. 5 then cuts diagonally to screen for No. 1 at the point. Player No. 3 throws a lob pass to No. 1 for a layup.

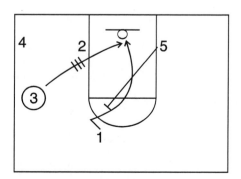

A

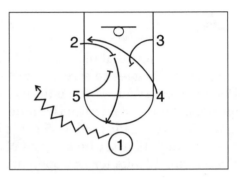

This is an attack that can be easily run at the end of the shot clock or as time is close to expiring. Player No. 1 dribbles to the wing as both No. 2 and No. 3 diagonally backscreen for No. 4 who cuts hard to the ballside block to post up. After No. 4 has cut, No. 5 turns and screens for No. 2 who will look for the jump shot.

B

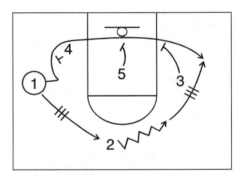

If No. 2 catches but cannot shoot, he will look for No. 1 cutting along the baseline as No. 1 receives three staggered screens to get open on the wing. (If No. 4, No. 5, or No. 3's defenders look to help on No. 1's cut, they should immediately turn toward the ball.)

This is the same initial box set and double backscreen as the previous play . The variation is the screen on the ball as the two screens are set.

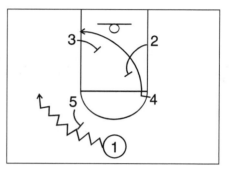

B

After No. 5 screens for No. 1, No. 5 turns and screens down for No. 2 who comes to the top of the circle for the jump shot.

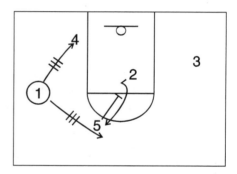

C

If No. 2 cannot catch the ball for the shot, both No. 2 and No. 5 screen away for No. 3.

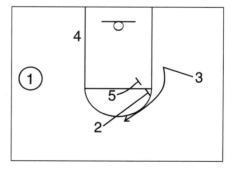

A

Player No. 1 enters the ball as No. 5 cuts to catch on the wing. Player No. 2 cuts opposite underneath a double screen set by No. 3 and No. 4. After No. 2 has cut, No. 3 curls around No. 4 into the lane.

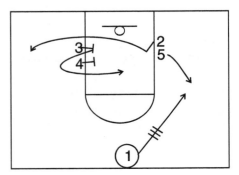

B

If No. 3 can't catch he continues to the ballside block. Player No. 1 then comes to screen for No. 4 who can either make a tight cut into the lane or flash to the free throw line.

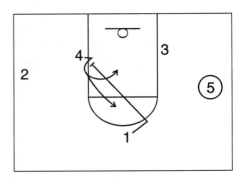

A

This is a very safe entry to being the offense. This low stack set condenses the defense and it is difficult for the defense to deny all the possible passing lanes.

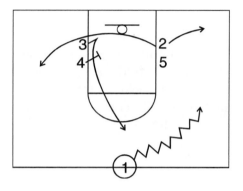

Here No. 1 dribbles the ball to the wing as No. 3 cuts up the lane to the top of the circle. Player No. 2 can cut to the ballside corner or cut opposite the ball underneath the screen set by No. 4.

B

As an option out of the entry here, No. 1 passes to No. 3 as No. 4 posts for a high/low pass and No. 1 screens for No. 4 for a curl cut. No. 2 stays wide for a perimeter shot if his defender helps.

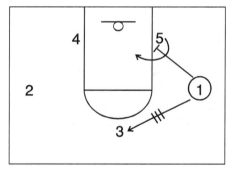

A

This double low stack set begins when No. 3 comes off of No. 4's screen to receive the pass from No. 1. After No. 3 receives the ball, No. 1 screens down for No. 5 who comes to the top of the circle.

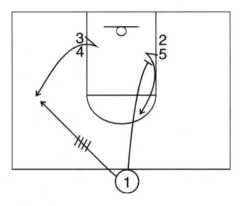

B

Player No. 3 reverses the ball to No. 5. After No. 5 receives the ball, both No. 4 and No. 3 screen for No. 1 who cuts across the lane looking for the jump shot. On the opposite side, No. 2 pops out to the wing.

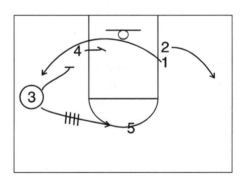

C

As an option, if the defense switches on the initial screen with X_1, switching out to No. 5 coming to the top of the circle, No. 1 reads the switch and immediately cuts underneath No. 4 to the corner for a jump shot.

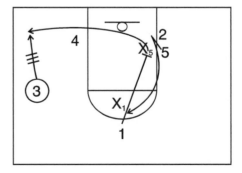

A

This is a set that attempts to spread out the defense. Player No. 1 dribbles to the wing as No. 3 sets his defender up then cuts under in the corner. Player No. 2 occupies his man until No. 5 screens for him. Player No. 2 must read the defense. Player No. 1 has numerous options: 1.) He can can penetrate to the basket, 2.) He can pass to No. 2 or No. 3 for jump shots, or 3.) He can pass to No. 4 for a post feed as No. 4 slides up the lane.

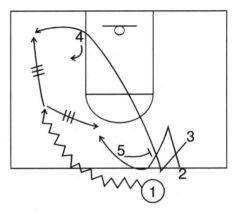

A

This is a good option out of the box set, especially if you have a 3-man who can post up as well as a 2-man who is capable of catching and shooting off of a downscreen. The ball is dribbled to the wing. Player No. 2 flashes off the double screen at the free-throw line. Player No. 4 flares to wing and receives the reversal pass from No. 2.

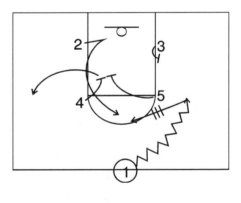

B

Double screen for No. 3 by both No. 5 and No. 2. If defense switches, dive the offensive player whose man has switched to the block.

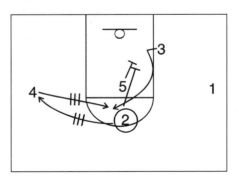

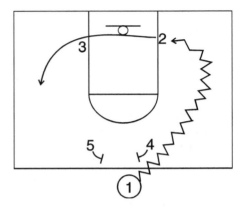

This play is out of a box set and is good for a team that has a point guard who is also a primary scorer. It is simple in that it doesn't involve any passing — only one other player may touch the ball. Both No. 4 and No. 5 come out on the floor to set a screen for No. 1. The side that No. 1 dribbles toward dictates which man at the block clears out. From here No. 1 attempts to penetrate to the basket or No. 1 and No. 4 can run a pick-and-roll.

A

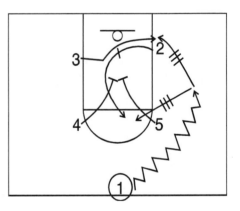

This is a very popular set and is used at every level that basketball is played. Player No. 1 dribbles the ball to the wing and No. 2 holds his spot on the ballside block to post. Player No. 2 then screens away for No. 3. Player No. 4 and No. 5 then screen down for No. 2 for the jump shot.

A

This particular set is good to run after a time out or as the first play of the half because the defense is usually excited to overplay at these points in the game. Player No. 1 dribbles to the wing and No. 4 downscreens for No. 3 who pops to the top of the circle and receives the ball. Player No. 2 then backscreens for No. 5 for a lob pass from No. 3.

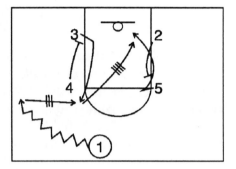

B

If the lob pass isn't open, No. 3 passes to No. 2 who has stepped back for a jump shot or a post feed to No. 5 who vigorously battles for post up position.

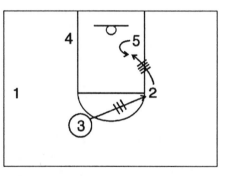

C

Option: Player No. 1 can pass to No. 3 who has read the defense and has cut to the corner for a possible baseline post fee to No. 4. From there into regular offense.

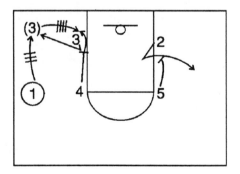

A

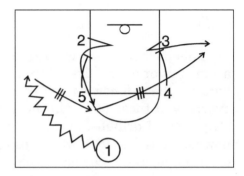

This is one of the standard options out of the box set. It is very effective if the offensive players are taught to read the defense as they come off of these initial screens. Player No. 1 dribbles the ball to the wing. Player No. 5 screens down for No. 2. The ball is reversed to No. 2. Player No. 2 looks inside for No. 5 posting up. Just as No. 2 is catching the ball, No. 4 screens down for No. 3 cutting flat along the baseline.

B

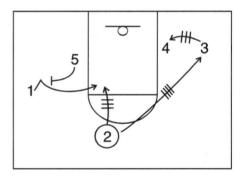

After No. 3 catches he looks for his shot. If he is covered, No. 3 looks to feed the post. If the ball cannot be reversed by No. 2 to No. 3, No. 5 steps out to screen for No. 1 who makes a curl cut into the lane.

A

Player No. 1 dribbles to the wing and No. 3 pops to the corner. Player No. 1 then reverses his dribble and receives a screen by No. 5 for a pick-and-roll. As No. 1 dribbles off of the screen by No. 5, No. 4 screens for No. 2 to create a two-man game for No. 2 on the wing and No. 4 posting up. Player No. 1 looks to "turn the corner" into the lane with the basketball as he dribbles off of No. 5's screen. This forces the defense to condense creating a penetration and pitch opportunity.

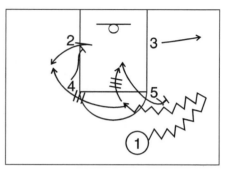

A

As in the previous play, No. 1 crosses the ball back to the middle of the floor from the wing. This time No. 3 stays in the block to receive either a downscreen from No. 5 or a double screen opposite low from No. 2 and No. 4. Player No. 1 shall be encouraged to penetrate into the lane to create help situations for the defense.

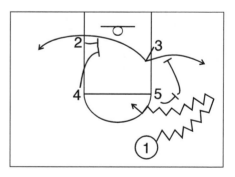

A

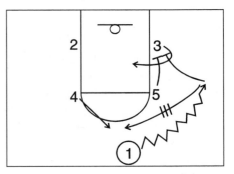

This is a nice counter play in the box alignment to the simple screen down. Player No. 1 takes the ball to the wing and No. 4 steps up from the elbow for ball reversal. Player No. 4 receives the pass from No. 1 and then both No. 5 and No. 1 set a double screen for No. 3 for a curl cut.

A

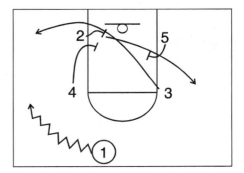

Player No. 4 and No. 2 set a double screen for No. 3 who cuts to the corner. Player No. 5 then screens for No. 2 who empties out across the lane opposite. If No. 1 passes to No. 3 in the corner, he can either shoot or look for No. 4 who will post up. If the ball is passed to No. 2, No. 5 can post up or No. 2 has the option to try to score.

Note: If No. 2's defender switches to No. 3 as No. 3 cuts off of this baseline double screen, No. 2 must next time screen.

A

This quick hitter is designed to create a mismatch for an inside player to post up. The goal is to have X_2 either have to switch onto No. 5, or to have X_2's help on No. 5's cut so No. 2 can be open for a shot at the top of the circle. Player No. 1 dribbles the ball to lane line extended and No. 2 diagonally upscreens for No. 4. Player No. 2 then steps up to catch the ball from No. 1. Player No. 2 can shoot if the opportunity presents itself.

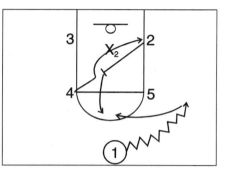

B

If No. 2 doesn't shoot the ball, No. 3 cuts to the corner and No. 5 dives to the opposite block looking to catch.

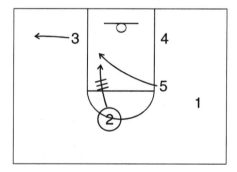

C

If the ball is reversed back to No. 1, he can take the ball on the dribble to No. 4 for a two man game.

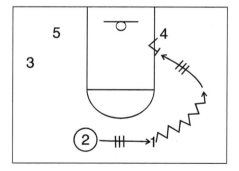

A

Player No. 1 dribbles the ball to the wing as No. 3 cuts underneath No. 4 along the baseline and as No. 5 screens in the middle of the lane for No. 2. If the ball is thrown to No. 3, he has the quick jump shot or baseline post feed to No. 4.

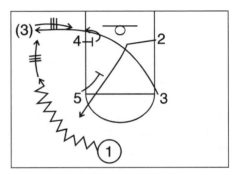

B

Player No. 1 passes to No. 2 for the jump shot. If the shot is not taken, No. 2 has two options: he can look for the cutter on the baseline screen as No. 4 screens for No. 3 for a possible layup, or No. 2 can dribble off of the screen set by No. 5 for the jump shot or pick-and-roll.

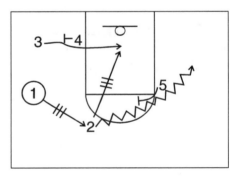

A

This is a very good quick hitter used after a time out or at the end of a game. Player No. 5 backscreens for No. 2 who flares out to the wing. At the same time No. 4 steps up and screens for No. 3 who cuts to the corner. After No. 5 screens No. 2 he steps to the ball to receive the basketball.

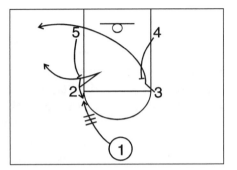

B

After No. 5 catches the ball, No. 4 sets a screen for No. 1 who flares to the wing for an isolation or for a quick pick-and-roll with No. 4.

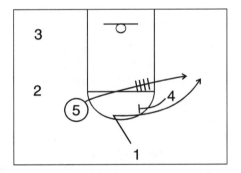

A

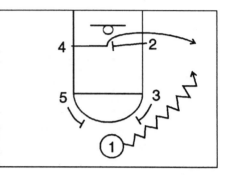

This is a good play if your team needs a 3-point basket because either the ball handler can shoot it or there will be an available shot after one pass. Players 3 and 5 screen for No. 1. The ball handler comes off of No. 3's screen looking for the shot or penetration into the lane. At the same time, No. 2 screens across the lane for No. 4. No. 4 continues out to the wing along the baseline.

B

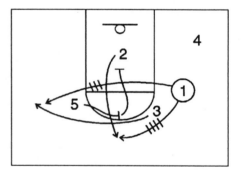

After No. 3 screens for No. 1, No. 5 immediately "picks-the-picker" and screens for No. 3 for the skip pass over the top of the defense. At the same time, No. 2 screens across the lane for No. 4. This puts No. 2 in position as the second option for the shot attempt. Player No. 1 skips the ball over the top of the defense to No. 3. After No. 5 screens for No. 3, he cuts down the lane to screen for No. 2 who comes to the top of the circle looking for the 3-point basket. If No. 3 is not open, No. 2 is a good second option for the shot.

A

Player No. 1 takes the ball to the wing as No. 5 screens across the free throw line for No. 3. Player No. 4 cuts to the ball side corner. Player No. 5 continues diagonally to screen again right away for No. 2 who makes a curl move into the lane for a short jump shot.

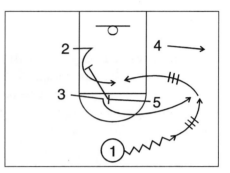

B

If X5 and X2 switch, No. 5 recognizes the mismatch and posts up quickly in the lane for a lob pass.

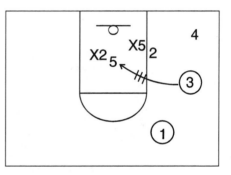

A

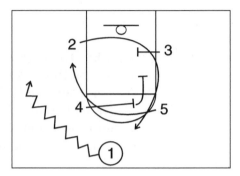

Player No. 1 brings the ball to the wing and No. 4 screens across for No. 5 who dives to the ballside block to post up. At the same time, No. 3 backscreens for No. 2 along the baseline. Player No. 2 also receives a second screen from No. 4. Here, player No. 2 is looking for a jump shot at the top of the arch.

B

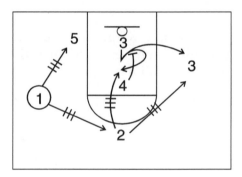

If No. 2 catches but is unable to get an open shot, he will look for No. 3 who has received a screen from No. 4. From here No. 3 must read his defender. Player No. 3 can make a curl cut or he can flare to the wing for a jump shot. Player No. 3 can also make a post feed to No. 4.

A

This quick hitter is intended to free an inside player who screens for a teammate and then steps to the ball. Player No. 1 brings the ball to the wing as No. 5 drops to the baseline to create a passing lane on the baseline. No. 2 moves from the weakside block and screens for No. 4. At the same time No. 3 sets a second screen for No. 4, No. 4 curls around into the lane. After No. 2 screens, he steps toward the ball.

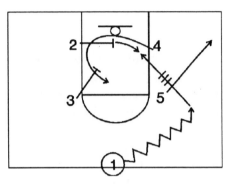

B

If No. 2's defender plays on the high side, No. 1 throws the ball to No. 5 for a baseline pass inside. Player No. 1 can also pass to No. 4 for a high/low pass. Player No. 3 flares to weakside wing to eliminate weakside help.

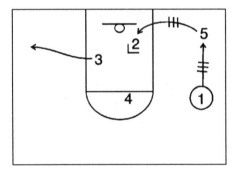

A

This alignment sets the bottom players wide on the wings which spreads the defense. Player No. 1 dribbles off of No. 5's screen; No. 4 then dives to the ballside block. After No. 5 screens for No. 1, he goes opposite to screen for No. 3. Player No. 2 slides toward the baseline creating space. If X4 defends the ball on the high side as No. 1 comes off of the screen set by No. 5, No. 1 passes to No. 2 for a potential post feed on the low side of the post defense.

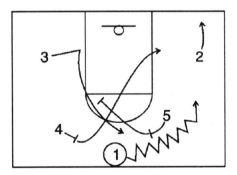

A

Player No. 1 takes the ball to the wing and No. 4 pops out to the lane line extended to receive No. 1's pass. Player No. 5 is looking to post up his defender as No. 1 has the ball at the wing. As No. 4 is catching the ball, No. 3 screens down for No. 2 who cuts hard to the wing looking for a jump shot. If their defenders switch, No. 3 looks to post his man up in the lane.

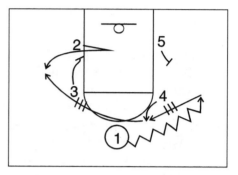

B

If No. 2 receives the ball on the wing but does not shoot, No. 3 will post up momentarily and then screen away for No. 5. Player No. 4 will then screen down for No. 3 who will look for the jump shot. Player No. 1 stays wide.

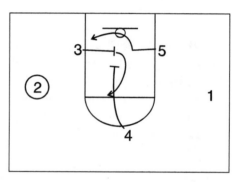

A

Player No. 1 takes the ball to the wing and No. 3 screens down for No. 2. Player No. 2 comes out to the wing. Player No. 3 then curls around the double screen set by No. 4 and No. 5 looking for short jump shot. If either No. 4 or No. 5's defenders switch or help on No. 3's curl, they should step to the ball.

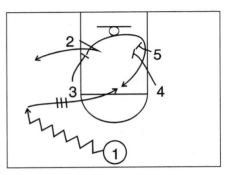

B

This is an option from the previous diagram. There is a ball screen added along with the pick-and-roll. Here No. 4 screens for No. 1 in the pick-and-roll as No. 2 receives a double screen for a jump shot. Player No. 3 flares to the corner as No. 5 reads weakside rebound or post up if No. 2 catches but can't shoot it.

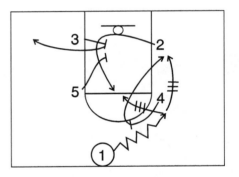

A

This is a "box set" with No. 4 and No. 5 set side by side. As No. 1 takes the ball to the wing, the man from the opposite block flashes to the top of the circle using No. 4 and No. 5 as screens. After No. 2 has received the pass, No. 4 pops out to the wing for ball reversal.

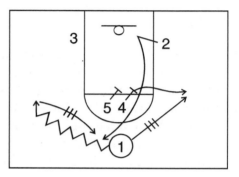

B

Player No. 2 and No. 5 double screen for No. 3. After No. 5 screens he turns back toward the ball.

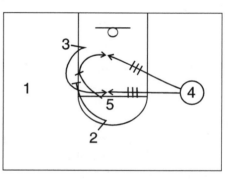

C

Option: As an option, if No. 2's defender trails this cutter then No. 2 circles around No. 4 and No. 5 and cuts right back to the hoop.

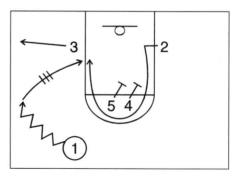

A

This is a variation of the previous play without the double screen. Player No. 3 receives the pass from No. 1 and reverses it to No. 4. Player No. 2 steps away from the lane to create space for himself.

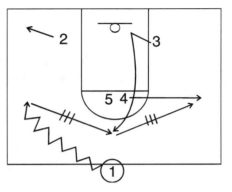

B

Now No. 5 goes to the opposite block to screen for No. 2 who reads the defense for either a baseline cut or a tight curl on the high side.

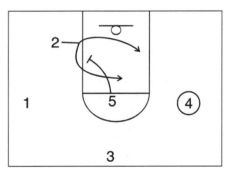

A

Player No. 1 takes the ball to the wing and both No. 5 and No. 4 set a double screen for No. 2 for a quick jump shot.

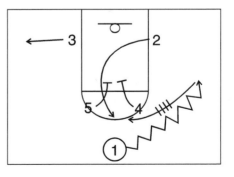

A

Player No. 2 and No. 3 pop to the wings and No. 1 passes to No. 2 and cuts to the corner.

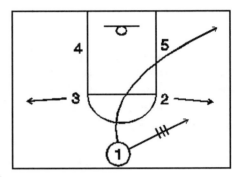

B

Player No. 4 flashes to the top of the circle for a pass from No. 2. Player No. 5 then posts up in the lane for a high/low pass from No. 4.

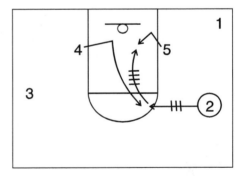

A

This is a simple isolation option that can be run to any player who possesses strong "post-up" abilities. Player No. 1 dribbles off of No. 4's screen as No. 3 pops to the corner. Player No. 1 can penetrate all the way if the opportunity presents itself. As No. 1 is using No. 4's screen, No. 5 is down screening for No. 2.

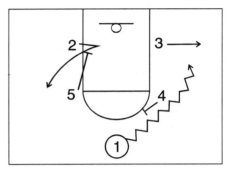

B

Player No. 1 reverses the ball back to No. 4 who looks inside for No. 5 isolated low.

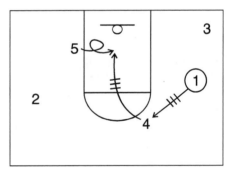

A

Player No. 1 takes the ball to the wing and No. 5 steps up to receive No. 1's pass. As soon as No. 5 catches, both No. 4 and No. 3 pop to the wing. Player No. 2 slides up the lane to force his defender to play post defense while also clearing out the baseline.

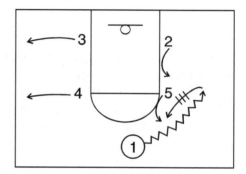

B

Player No. 5 reverses the ball to No. 4 and No. 2 backscreens for No. 5. If No. 2's defender does not help on No. 5's cut, the lob pass will be available.

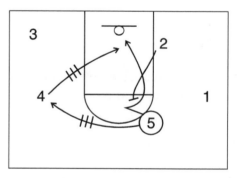

C

If No. 5 does not receive the lob pass, No. 2 steps back to receive the ball from No. 4. Player No. 5 turns in the lane and seals his man off either for a lob pass or a direct pass from No. 2.

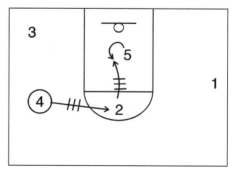

A

Player No. 4 screens for No. 1 as they look for a pick-and-roll or perhaps No. 1 can go all the way to the hoop when he turns the corner off of No. 4's pick. Player No. 2 and No. 3 get wide to spread the defense. Player No. 5 rotates up to the top of the circle.

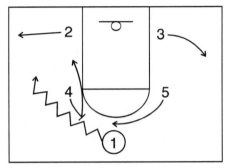

B

As No. 4's defender has fought hard to deny the pick-and-roll by perhaps playing three-quarters around No. 4 or momentarily fronting him, No. 4 stays at the midpost level of the lane allowing the defender to choose how he will defend him. Player No. 1 then reverses the ball to No. 5 and No. 4 seals his defender for a high/low entry pass into the lane.

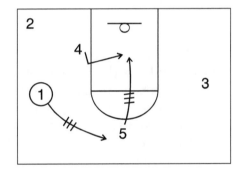

A

Player No. 1 dribbles to No. 2's side and No. 2 cuts across the lane as if to set a screen for No. 4. Player No. 5 holds his spot until No. 2 backscreens for him. At the same time, No. 4 backscreens for No. 3 who flares to the wing for the jump shot.

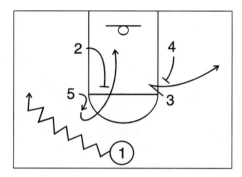

B

Player No. 1 passes to No. 2 who, if open, will have the jump shot. The other option is No. 5 who seals his defender and looks for the lob pass or, if the defense is caught behind No. 5 there is a direct pass into the lane. A post player's delight!

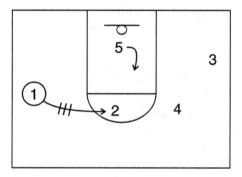

A

This is a good play to run after a time out especially if possession time is limited.

Players No. 3 and No. 5 downscreen. Player No. 4 cuts to the ballside corner drawing the defender out also. Player No. 2 finds a passing angle at the top of the key in case the ball needs to be reversed.

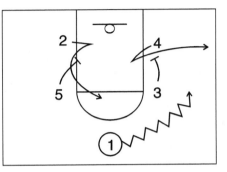

B

After No. 3 screens for No. 4 the action is continuous as No. 3 immediately screens across the lane for No. 5.

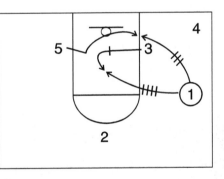

C

Option: As an option to the previous set, if the ball is brought to No. 5's side of the floor the same action takes place except that after No. 5 screens across the lane for No. 3, he reverse pivots and seals his defender in the lane. A lob pass is thrown to No. 5 over X5, who is caught between the ball and No. 5.

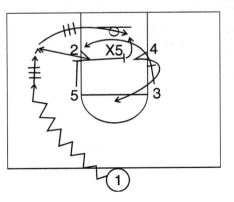

A

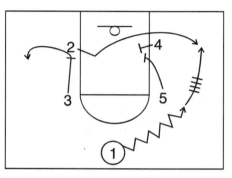

Player No. 2 is your primary scorer. Player No. 4 and No. 5 stack up on the opposite side of the lane as No. 3 sets a downscreen then cuts to the corner thus spreading the defense. Player No. 2 cuts underneath both No. 4 and No. 5's screens. Player No. 1 passes to No. 2 for a quick jump shot.

B

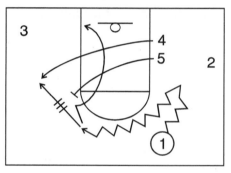

Option: After No. 2 has passed under the double screen but has not received the ball, No. 4 continues to the opposite wing. Player No. 1 changes direction with his dribble and passes to No. 4. Player No. 5 screens for No. 1 for a shuffle cut and a possible layup.

C

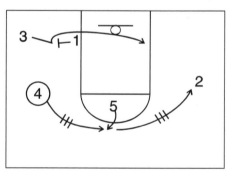

Player No. 4 reverses the ball through No. 5 to No. 2. Player No. 1 backscreens for No. 3. Player No. 4 and No. 5 double screen for No. 1 for a jump shot.

A

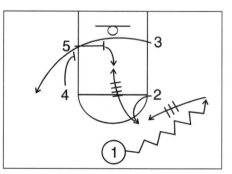

This play begins in a box set. Player No. 1 takes the ball to the wing as No. 2 steps up to the top of the circle. Player No. 5 then screens across the lane for No. 3, and No. 4 sets a second screen. After No. 5 screens, he steps to the ball.

Box Continuity Offense

A

This offense has become very popular recently and has numerous options within its pattern. It begins in a box set with the 4 and 5 man at the free-throw line and the 2 and 3 at each block. The two big men pop out to the wings; No. 1 passes to No. 5 and screens away for No. 4. As No. 4 and No. 5 are cutting to the wings, No. 2 and No. 3 are cutting up to the free-throw line. Once the ball has been passed to a side, the ball side man on the block goes hard to corner while the weakside block player comes over the ballside elbow.

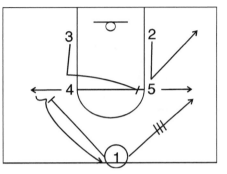

B

Player No. 5 reverses the ball to No. 4, who in turn reverses it to No. 1. Player No. 5 holds his spot on the wing until No. 4 releases the ball to No. 1. Player No. 3 sets a shuffle cut screen at the elbow for No. 5, and No. 4 screens for No. 3 for a jump shot at the top of the key.

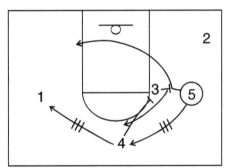

C

Player No. 1 now has two options, he can pass to No. 5 for the layup or the No. 3 for the jump shot.

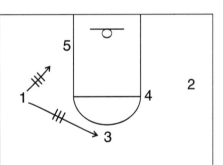

D

If No. 1 passes to No. 3 but No. 3 does not attempt a shot, No. 5 backscreens for No. 1 and No. 4 sets another screen in the lane. Player No. 4 steps to the ball after his screen is set.

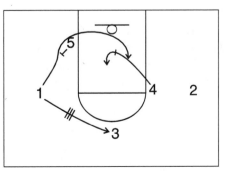

Option

A

One option starts with the point to wing pass and screen away. Here No. 4 replaces No. 1 at the point after No. 1 picks away from the ball.

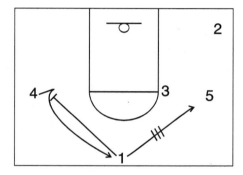

B

Here No. 4 dribbles No. 1 off the wing as No. 3 screens for No. 5 on the weak side. Player No. 1 screen for No. 5 who looks to post up.

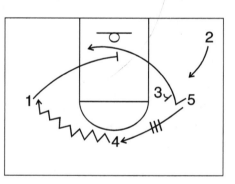

C

After No. 1 screens for No. 5 (Diagram B), both No. 3 and No. 2 look to set a double screen for No. 1 coming up the middle of the lane for a pass from No. 4.

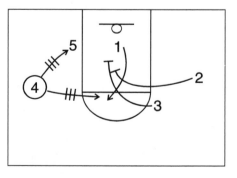

Option

A

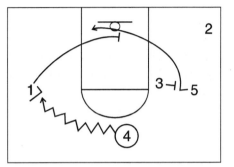

Player No. 4 has the ball at the top of the circle, but can't reverse the ball to No. 1 because No. 1's defender is denying the wing pass. Player No. 5 cuts off of No. 3 and receives a second screen from No. 1.

B

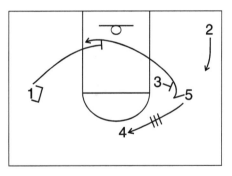

As soon as No. 5 has cut and No. 2 sees that the ball cannot be reversed to No. 1, No. 2 moves up to the free-throw line extended to receive a pass from No. 4.

C

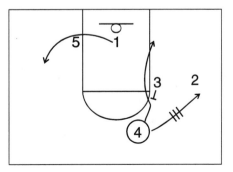

As soon as No. 4 passes to No. 2, No. 3 sets a screen at the free-throw line for No. 4. Player No. 1 empties out underneath No. 5 to the opposite wing for spacing purposes and for possible ball reversal.

Option

A

Player No. 1 passes to No. 4 and No. 1 cuts away but replaces himself back on the point.

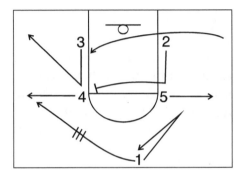

B

Player No. 4 passes the ball back to No. 4 and No. 1 dribbles the ball toward No. 5. When No. 5 sees the ball coming toward him, he cuts toward the basket and posts up.

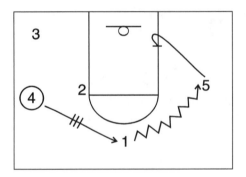

C

Player No. 1 takes the ball to about the free-throw line extended for a low post feed. At the same time, No. 2 screens for No. 4 as he cuts to the basket. Player No. 3 cuts right behind No. 4 as No. 3 cuts toward the inside of the top of the circle for the jump shot.

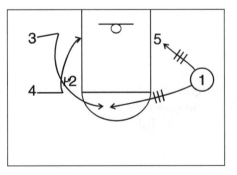

Option

A

Player No. 1 changes his direction with his dribble as No. 4 screens down for No. 3. Player No. 3 pops out to the wing looking for the pass.

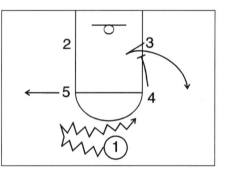

B

At this point No. 3 reverse pivots and No. 4 and No. 3 both double screen for No. 2 along the baseline.

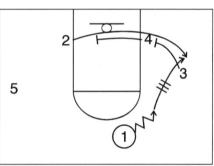

C

If No. 1 can't pass the ball to No. 2, No. 4 comes out to receive a pass from No. 1. Player No. 4 swings the ball to No. 5.

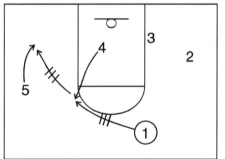

D

Once No. 5 catches the ball, No. 3 backscreens for No. 2 along the baseline. After one or two optional cuts out of this initial set, the 1-4 offense can easily flow into a single post or double post passing game.

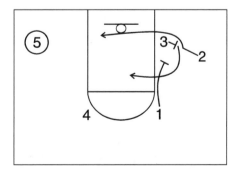

Option

A

Both No. 4 and No. 5 pop out to their wing and both No. 2 and No. 3 cut hard up the lane lines to the free-throw line. Player No. 1 passes to No. 3.

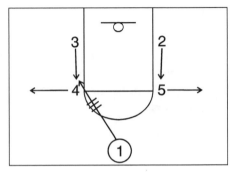

B

As soon as No. 3 receives the pass, No. 4 cuts to the ballside block and looks to post up for a high/low pass from No. 3. Player No. 3 may take a dribble or two out to the wing to improve his passing angle to the block. Player No. 2 backscreens for No. 1 and No. 3 looks for the skip pass to No. 1. When No. 1 catches the skip pass he can shoot or look to throw the ball into the low post to No. 5.

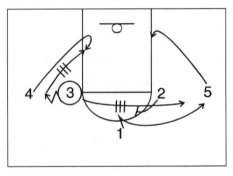

C

If No. 5 does not receive a pass from No. 1, he turns and screens away for No. 4. Player No. 2 screens away for No. 3 also.

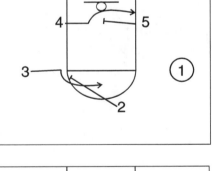

D

Another option in this set once the ball comes to No. 3 is to have No. 2 slide down the lane line and screen for No. 5 who makes a baseline cut into the lane.

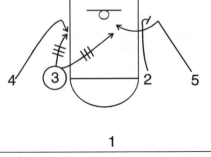

A

Another series of options begins with No. 1 passing to No. 4 and cutting to the ballside corner.

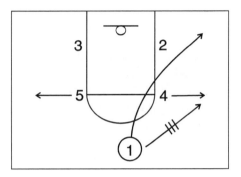

B

Once No. 4 has received the ball, No. 5 cuts directly across the free-throw line to the ballside high post and No. 2 cuts directly behind him to the lane line extended. This should be timed so that No. 5 and No. 2's cuts are simultaneous.

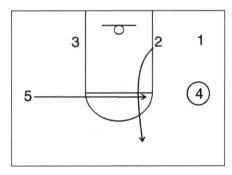

C

Player No. 4 looks to No. 1 to see if No. 1's defender is overplaying the passing lane. Player No. 4 takes two or three dribbles toward the top of the circle as No. 1 extends his defender further toward the sideline. Player No. 4 reverse pivots and No. 1 then breaks to the basket. When No. 5 sees No. 4 dribble, he turns to clear out so No. 4 has room for the backdoor pass.

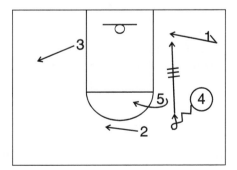

D

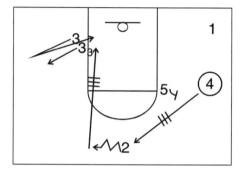

Another option is having No. 4 pass to No. 2 who dribbles toward the other wing. As No. 2 dribbles toward No. 3's side, No. 3 cuts hard to the wing to catch the ball. If No. 3's defender denies the pass on the wing, No. 3 backcuts to the basket for a pass from No. 2.

E

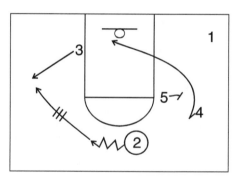

While No. 3 receives the ball on the wing, No. 4 is making his cut off of No. 5. After No. 3 receives the pass, he looks into No. 4 at the block for a possible post feed.

F

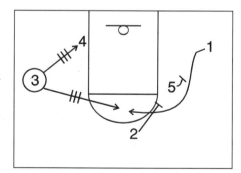

Once No. 3 receives the ball, his first option is to look to score himself. His second option is to make the post feed to No. 4 or pass to No. 1 for a score as both No. 5 and No. 2 set a double screen for No. 1, who makes a curl cut. If No. 2 takes the dribble to the wing, No. 3 empties out and will screen for No. 4 in the middle of the lane. Player No. 5 will turn and come down the middle of the lane looking to pick No. 3, a pick the picker triangle action in the lane.

A

This is a special play out of the box continuity offense designed for a last second two-point or three-point field goal attempt. Player No. 4 reverses the ball to No. 1. Player No. 5 steps toward No. 3 as if to receive his screen, but No. 3 curls back and cuts hard diagonally attempting to make his cut in front of his defender in order to catch the ball for a layup.

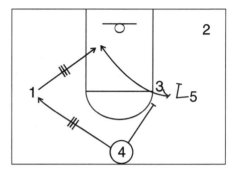

B

After No. 3 makes his cut both No. 5 and No. 4 turn to screen for No. 2 who is coming off those screens for a jump shot — if you team needs a three-point basket, this is where you will get the opportunity.

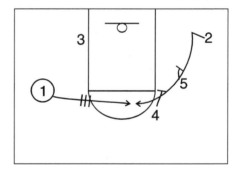

A

This is another little special that can be run if the defense is denying the big men the ball out on the wing. Both No. 4 and No. 5 cross out at the free-throw line. Even if these defenders switch to deny No. 4 and No. 5, that's all right because No. 1 passes the ball to No. 2 as the wings are wide.

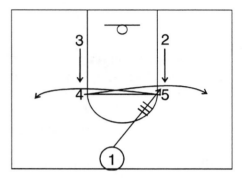

B

As soon as No. 2 receives the pass from the point, No. 4 cuts backdoor for a layup. Player No. 2 turns to the outside and feeds No. 4.

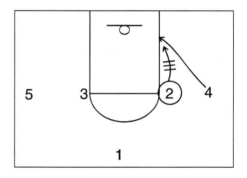

Tight Stack Sets

A

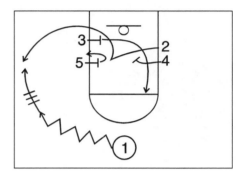

This is a tight stack along the baseline and can be run to either side. Here No. 1 dribbles the ball to the left wing. Player 2 runs underneath the double screen set by No. 3 and No. 5. After No. 2 cuts past No. 3's shoulder No. 4 screens in the lane for No. 3. Player 3 goes opposite the ball looking to create a passing lane for himself and No. 1. If No. 2 receives the ball in the corner he can shoot or look inside to No. 5 posting up for the ball.

B

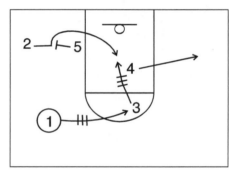

If the ball is reversed crosscourt to No. 3, No. 5 backscreens for No. 2 who quickly reverses his direction to screen his defender again along the baseline. Here No. 3 looks inside for No. 2 getting a layup.

C

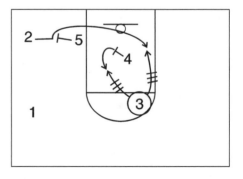

As an option, No. 4 can set a double screen for No. 2. Now two potential receivers are looking for the ball in the lane.

A

This is a double stack set as No. 3 cuts underneath the double attempting to get open on the wing. Player No. 1 brings the ball to No. 3's cut.

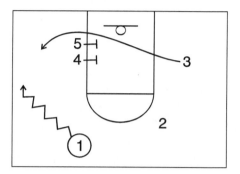

B

After No. 4 screens in the stack set, this player will pop up the lane to receive a pass from No. 1. The ball is reversed to No. 4, and No. 5 immediately turns and screens for No. 3 who makes a shuffle cut back into the lane looking for a layup.

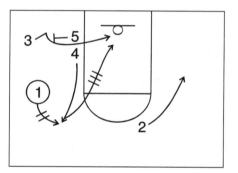

A

This is a single stack set out of a two guard front. Player No. 1 passes to No. 2 and then No. 1 cuts away from the ball to set up his defender. Player No. 5 then steps up to screen for No. 1 who makes a diagonal cut to the open wing. Player No. 1 now looks to go 1-on-1 on his open side.

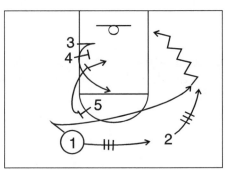

B

At the same time, No. 4 screens in for No. 3 who can flare or curl. Player No. 5 also looks to screen for No. 3 and then No. 5 steps to the ball.

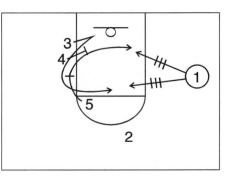

A

This features the same alignment as the previous diagram but a dribble entry can start this set. Player No. 1 dribbles to the wing as No. 2 cuts off of No. 4's screen up at the high post.

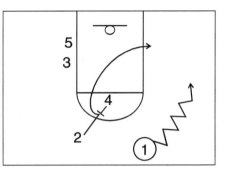

B

Player No. 4 then looks to receive the pass from No. 1 inside the top of the circle. Player No. 2 makes a curl cut around the stack looking for the layup or short jump shot from No. 4's pass.

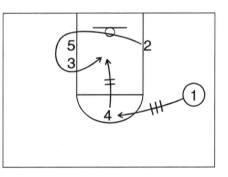

C

If No. 2 makes his curl but does not receive the pass, No. 5 curls right behind No. 2 as No. 2's cut will sometimes decoy the defense for the second cutter. As in this diagram, No. 5 is the second cutter for the pass from No. 4.

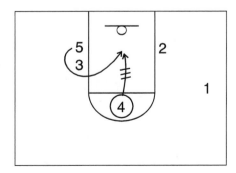

A

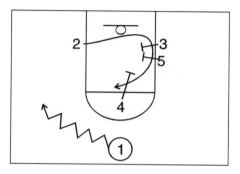

This play begins with a single stack set and a one guard front. Player No. 1 dribbles the ball to No. 2's side, No. 2 empties out behind the double screen set by No. 3 and No. 5. There may be a skip pass available to No. 2 if No. 2's defender gets caught in the lane on the double screen. Player No. 4 sets his downscreen to free No. 2.

B

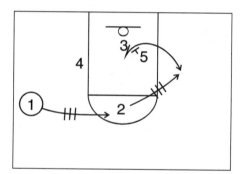

Player No. 1 hits No. 2 for a jump shot. Player No. 5 screens again on No. 3's man as No. 3 flares to corner. Player No. 1 has the secondary option of throwing a skip pass to No. 3. After No. 4 screens for No. 2, he steps toward No. 1 looking for a quick pass.

Stack
Sets

A

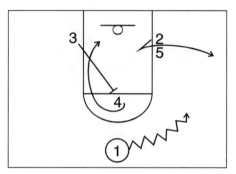

This offense originates out of a single stack set. It is effective offense for a team that has only one effective outside shooter. In these diagrams consider No. 3 as the best outside threat. Player No. 1 takes the ball to the stack side and No. 2 pops to the wing after receiving No. 5's screen. Player No. 3 backscreens for No. 4 and immediately looks for the ball to score.

B

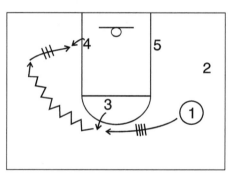

If No. 3 catches but doesn't attempt a shot, the ball is taken to the wing for a two man game.

C

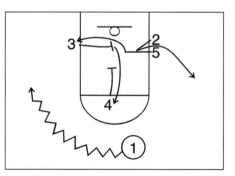

If No. 1 takes the ball to No. 3's side, No. 3 turns to screen for No. 5 in the lane and No. 4 will screen down for No. 3 for the jump shot. Player No. 2 gets wide on the weak side for a skip pass.

D

Another option with No. 1 taking the ball to No. 3's side is having No. 4 screen down for No. 3. Also, rather than a downscreen, No. 3 can also backscreen No. 4's defender and then pop out for the jump shot.

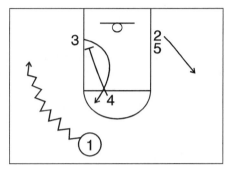

E

Player No. 1 takes the ball away for No. 3 and both No. 5 and No. 4 screen for No. 2. Player No. 2 can go either way to receive No. 1's pass. If No. 2 catches the ball off of No. 4's screen, No. 3 cuts hard out to the wing. If No. 3 is overplayed, he can go backdoor for a layup.

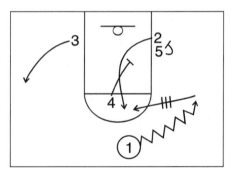

A

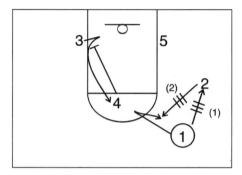

Player No. 1 takes the ball to the stack side and passes to No. 2. Player No. 1 receives the return pass as No. 4 down-screens for No. 3.

B

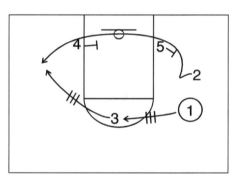

Player No. 3 receives the pass from No. 1 as No. 3 is positioned a little wider than lane line extended. Player No. 2 then cuts hard along the baseline taking two staggered screens from both No. 5 and No. 4. Player No. 2 looks for the jump shot when he receives the pass.

A

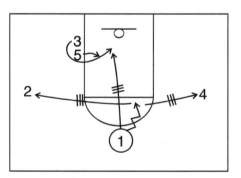

This is a quick hitter out of a stack set. Player No. 3 curls around No. 5 and looks for No. 1's pass. After No. 3 curls, No. 5 stops into the lane behind No. 3's cut because No. 5's defender will help to defend No. 3 in the lane. Player No. 1 can penetrate and pitch because the defense is spread out on the wings as well as flattened on the baseline.

A

Here No. 4 screens on the ball as No. 2 receives a double screen from No. 3 and No. 5. Player No. 3 is looking for a postup or a jump shot along the baseline.

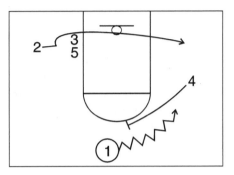

B

If No. 2 does not receive the pass from No. 1, the ball is reversed to No. 4. After No. 4 receives the pass, No. 5 turns and screens for No. 3 who is the low man in the stack set. Here No. 3 must read the defense: he can pop to the wing (as shown) or he can curl into the lane or flare parallel to the baseline to the corner. After No. 5 screens for No. 3, he is also looking for a pass from No. 4.

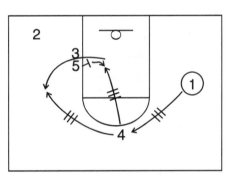

C

After No. 3 receives No. 4's pass he looks to shoot, drive or post feed to No. 5 inside.

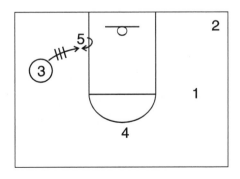

D

Another option off of the stack set is No. 2 cutting underneath both No. 3 and No. 5. Here No. 2 enters the lane, but is successfully defended. Here No. 2 curls back out of the lane screening his defender a second time.

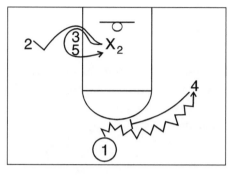

E

The ball is reversed by No. 1 to No. 4. Player No. 4 looks inside as No. 2 curls underneath the stack back into the lane. After No. 2 curls into the lane, No. 3 follows No. 2 into the lane.

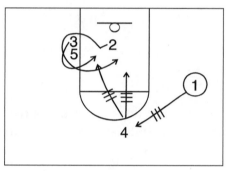

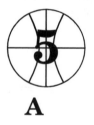

A

This is a single stack set as No. 1 dribbles off of No. 5's screen. If No. 1 can penetrate into the lane, he does so. Player No. 3 cuts off of No. 4's screen looking for a jump shot.

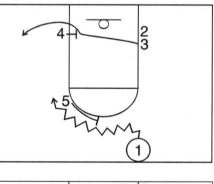

B

After No. 5 screens for No. 1, No. 2 backscreens for No. 5 for a lob pass.

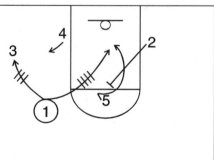

A

This is a good "last-second" play. Player No. 1 gets a screen above the top of the key. Everyone else is flattened out along the baseline to give No. 1 some room to penetrate. Player No. 1 passes to No. 3 in the corner. Player No. 2 screens for No. 4 along the base. Player No. 4 is looking for a layup here. Player No. 5 downscreens for No. 2 who looks for the jump shot.

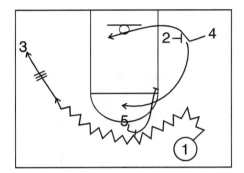

A

Player No. 2 goes down the lane and screens for No. 4. Player No. 4 receives the pass from No. 1 and then looks inside as No. 3 curls around No. 5 for a short jump shot in the lane or even a layup!

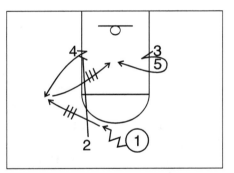

B

If X2 and X4 switch and X2 is successful in denying the pass to No. 4 on the wing, No. 2 immediately reads the defense and cuts underneath the stack set and looks for a pass from No. 1. After No. 2 has cleared the double screen, No. 3 curls into the lane looking for the ball.

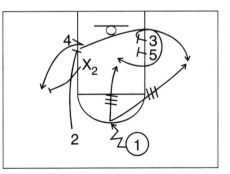

A

This play is out of a 2-3 set and it looks to isolate some perimeter people inside while also creating a two man game with a perimeter scorer with a post player. Player No. 1 passes to No. 4 and follows his pass for a hand off. At this point both No. 3 and No. 5 set a double screen on the weakside block.

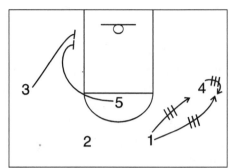

B

After No. 4 hands the ball back to No. 1, No. 4 then steps up to the top of the circle to screen No. 2's defender. This will momentarily clear out the side of the floor for No. 2 who cuts hard looking for a pass from No. 1.

C

If No. 2 doesn't receive the ball, No. 1 reverses the ball through No. 4. Upon No. 4's catch No. 3 uses a screen by No. 5 to free himself on the block. No. 3 must read the defense. A curl cut back into the lane might be available. No. 1 screens down for No. 2 on the other side. If 1's defender is going to switch onto 2 as he cuts to the wing, tell 1 to screen his own defender, X. This will free 2 on the wing for the catch.

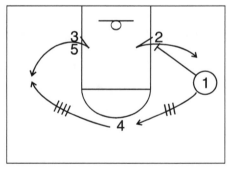

D

Once No. 3 has received the ball, No. 3 must look inside for the two man game; No. 5 might be open for a post feed. Player No. 4 screens away for No. 2 who makes a middle cut down the lane for a possible layup from a pass from No. 3 or No. 5.

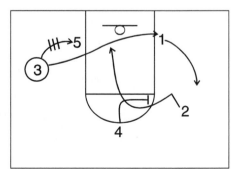

A

Player No. 1 passes the ball to No. 4 who has stepped out on the perimeter. Player No. 4 reverses the ball to No. 3. After No. 3 has received the ball, No. 5 cuts hard across the lane to post up ball side. At the same time both No. 4 and No. 1 double screen for No. 2.

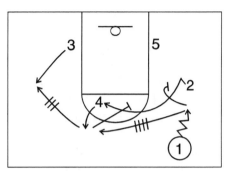

A

Player No. 4 cuts to the wing and receives the pass from No. 1. Player No. 5 then cuts across the lane to post up as No. 1 cuts to the ballside corner.

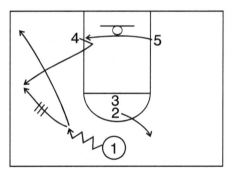

B

Player No. 4 then passes to No. 2. Player No. 3 screens for No. 4 as No. 4 shuffle cuts into the lane looking for a pass from No. 2.

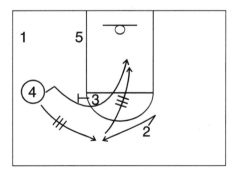

A

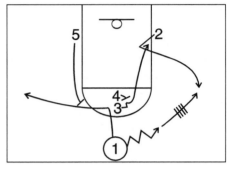

Player No. 3 and No. 4 are stacked at the free-throw line while No. 5 and No. 2 are in the low post area. Player No. 1 passes to No. 2 who cut to the wing to begin the offense. After No. 2 catches the ball on the wing, No. 4 screens for No. 3 who cuts toward the basket looking for a pass from No. 2. After No. 1 passes to No. 2, No. 5 comes up the lane and backscreens for No. 1 for a possible skip pass.

B

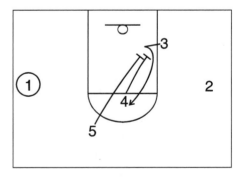

After No. 5 screens he steps up to receive a reversal pass from No. 2. Player No. 5 then passes to No. 1.

C

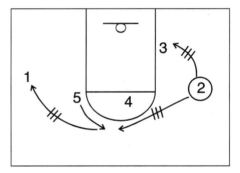

After No. 1 has received the pass, both No. 4 and No. 5 set a double screen for No. 3 who cuts looking for the jump shot. Note: If No. 5 can't pass the ball to No. 1, No. 5 can return the ball back to No. 2, and No. 4 and No. 5 can screen away for No. 1.

D

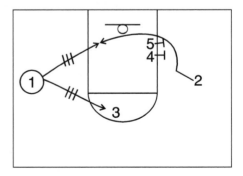

Player No. 1 has the ball on the wing but did not pass the ball to No. 3 for the jump shot. The next option is No. 4 and No. 5 setting the double screen for No. 2 who cuts across the lane looking for a layup.

High Post Offense

A

Player No. 1 passes to No. 4 and cuts to the ballside corner. Player No. 5 posts up strong looking for position. Player No. 3, who is at the high post feels his defender overplaying in an attempt to deny the high-post pass. Player No. 3 reverse pivots and rolls to the hoop for a lob pass.

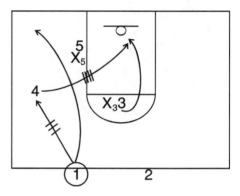

A

Player No. 1 passes to No. 4 and cuts and replaces. Player No. 4 passes to No. 3 who catches and pivots toward the basket. Player No. 2 cuts through the lane to screen for No. 5. Player No. 5 looks for the high/low pass from the free-throw line. After No. 2 screens for No. 5, he continues out to the wing as No. 4 screens down for him.

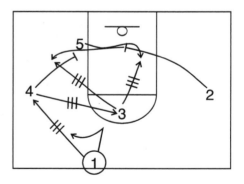

A

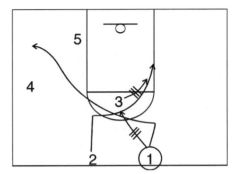

This is a "clear-out" play for one of the guards after the guards split off of the high post. Player No. 1 passes the ball to No. 3 and cuts off the high post first. Player No. 2 follows as the second cutter with the side cleared out for a layup. If No. 5's defender helps on the penetration, No. 2 gives No. 5 a quick pass for a layup.

A

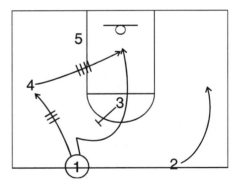

This is a lob play for one of the guards as No. 1 passes to No. 4 and makes a quick cut off the high post for a lob pass for No. 4. This is a nice option to run after a time-out.

A

Player No. 1 passes to No. 3 who turns to face the basket. Player No. 4 sets his defender up with a "V-cut" and cuts hard into the lane off of No. 5's screen. Both No. 1 and No. 2 widen out to the wings to spread the defense and to spot up for jump shots.

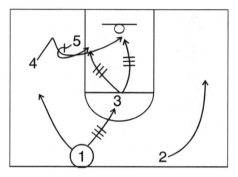

A

This is another entry for the lob to the high post man except No. 1 dribbles No. 4 from the wing down to the baseline. Now No. 3 spins and looks quickly for the lob pass. If No. 3 catches the ball at the high post, No. 4 is in position for No. 5's baseline screen.

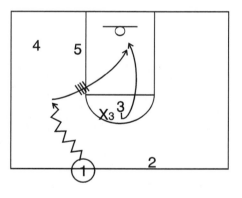

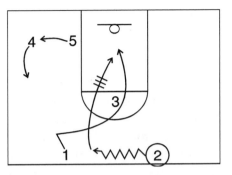

A

In this situation, No. 2 dribbles toward No. 1 and makes a cut over No. 3's screen looking for a lob.

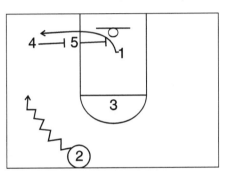

B

If No. 1 doesn't get the lob, there are still a number of options such as both No. 4 and No. 5 setting staggered screens for No. 1 to come out on the wing;

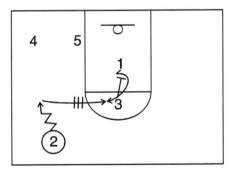

C

Or No. 3 can turn and screen again down the middle of the lane for No. 1.

A

In a double screen option, No. 1 passes to the wing and No. 3 spins looking for a possible lob pass from No. 4. Player No. 1 cuts through to the opposite block. Player No. 5 cuts up the lane to the free-throw line for a pass from No. 4.

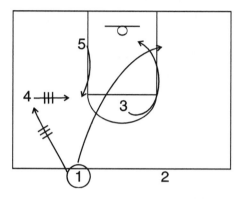

B

As No. 5 is catching the ball, No. 2 times his cut for a handoff or shovel pass as he cuts over No. 5.

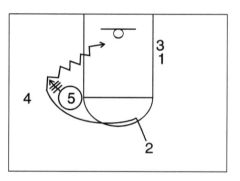

C

If No. 2 does not receive the ball from No. 5, No. 2 continues under the double screen set by No. 3 and No. 1.

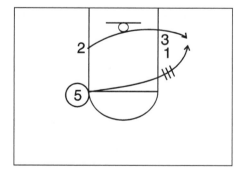

A

If No. 1 passes to the wing and cuts to the corner, No. 4 looks to No. 3 at the high post. After No. 3 receives the pass, No. 1 cuts off of No. 5's screen for a high/low pass and a layup. After No. 5 screens, he turns back to the ball for a pass if his man helps on No. 1's cut.

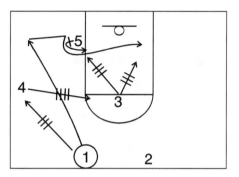

B

After No. 1 has cut to the corner, another option is to have No. 4 throw the ball back to No. 1 and cut through. After No. 1 receives the ball, No. 5 comes out to set a screen on the ball. Here they run a pick-and-roll.

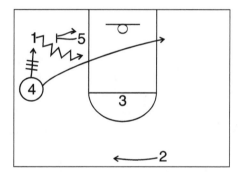

A

Another double screen option for one of the guards is to have No. 1 pass to No. 4 at the wing. As soon as No. 1 has passed to No. 4, No. 5 empties out across the lane on the opposite block. Player No. 2 cuts off of the high post looking for a layup off of No. 3's screen at the free-throw line. Player No. 3 goes opposite the ball to stack up with No. 5.

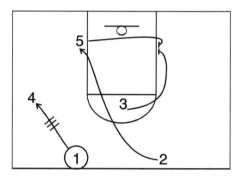

B

Player No. 1 has cut and replaced himself. Player No. 4 reverses the ball back to No. 1 and he dribbles the ball into position to be able to pass the ball to No. 2 as he curls around the double stack.

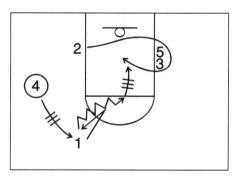

A

Player No. 1 passes to No. 3 at the high post and then screens for No. 2 who, in turn, looks for a quick pass from No. 3 for a jump shot. If the split by the guards doesn't break down the defense, No. 3 turns and looks for No. 4 taking the baseline screen from No. 5. If No. 4's defender switches, No. 5 turns back to the ball for a layup.

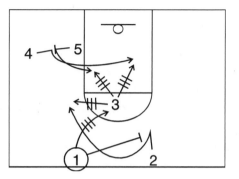

B

This play will produce a quick opening for No. 3 as he will get a short jump shot. Player No. 1 passes to No. 4 as No. 5 quickly empties out from the ballside block across the lane. Player No. 1 make his cut as if he is going toward the corner, then pivots and screens for No. 3 who curls around the screen for a quick pass from No. 4.

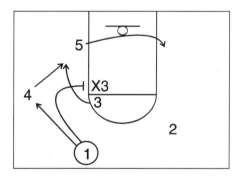

A

Player No. 1 dribbles the ball toward No. 4 and passes the ball to No. 3 at the high post. Player No. 5 steps wide of the lane to take his defender away from the basket as No. 3 turns and pivots toward No. 2 who cuts to the basket for a layup.

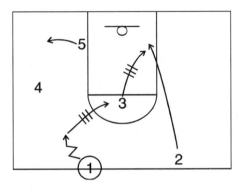

A

This is another pick-and-roll option as No. 1 passes to No. 4 and cuts to the ball-side corner. Player No. 5 goes to the opposite block as No. 4 passes to No. 1 in the corner. After No. 4 passes, he cuts off of No. 3 at the high post. Player No. 2 rotates over toward the ball for a passing angle.

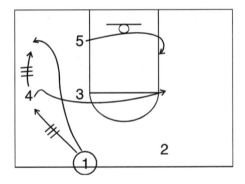

B

Player No. 3 comes out to the corner to screen on the ball for a pick-and-roll. This is a good play in that the position of the screen on the floor makes the defense very vulnerable if they fail to defend it properly — one or two dribbles or a quick pass to No. 3 results in a layup or short jump shot.

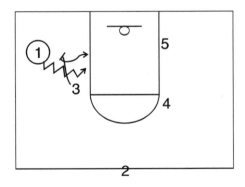

A

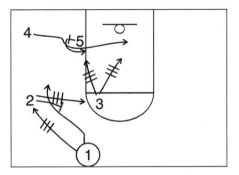

Player No. 1 passes to No. 2 but No. 1 holds his spot until No. 2 passes the ball to No. 3. Player No. 3 turns and looks for No. 4 cutting over No. 5's screen, if No. 4 is open, he gets a layup; No. 5 turns back to the ball if his defender helps or switches then. No. 5 gets a layup. The second option is No. 2 screening for No. 1 who, if No. 1 received the ball, has the whole side of the court.

A

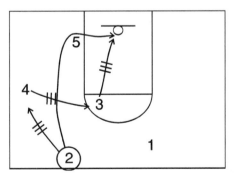

Player No. 2 passes to No. 4 and cuts toward the corner. Player No. 4 passes to No. 3 at the high post; No. 3 then turns and looks for No. 2 as No. 5 backscreens for No. 2 for the cut into the lane and a layup.

A

This is a very useful option that can create a mismatch inside. Player No. 1 dribbles to the wing and passes to No. 3 at the high post. Player No. 1 then continues across the lane and screens for No. 5. Player No. 3 looks inside for the pass to No. 5. Player No. 2 follows No. 1 to the wing for a possible passing angle if No. 3 cannot feed No. 5 from the free-throw line. Player No. 2 is then in position to pass to No. 5 along the baseline.

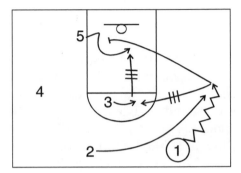

B

If No. 5 can't receive the pass from No. 3 (Diagram above), No. 4 screens down for No. 1 for a shot on the opposite wing.

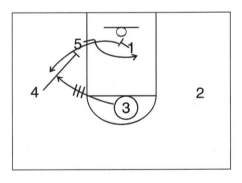

A

Player No. 4 screens above the top of the circle for No. 1. As No. 1 dribbles past the screen, No. 3 pops to the wing to be a potential receiver and to spread the defense for penetration by the ballhandler. Player No. 5 follows the direction of the ball going from block to block. Player No. 2 immediately screens No. 4's defender for a lob pass after No. 4's screen.

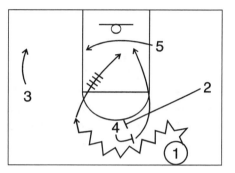

B

If the lob pass can't be thrown by No. 1, the ball is reversed to No. 2 for a quick 2-man game with No. 4 posting up.

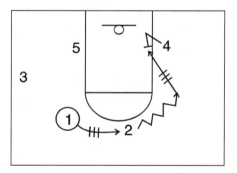

Option

A

Player No. 1 dribbles off of No. 4's screen as No. 2 runs the baseline underneath No. 5's screen. After No. 4 screens for No. 1, No. 3 screens No. 4's defender. Player No. 4 rolls to the loop looking for a lob pass.

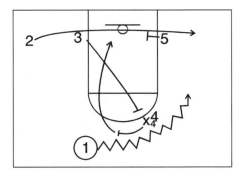

B

Here No. 1 throws the ball to No. 2 who looks for a possible shot. If that scoring opportunity doesn't present itself, No. 2 looks inside for a baseline feed to No. 5. Player No. 4 on the weakside block must reposition himself either up the lane or off of the block along the baseline. This eliminates No. 4's defender from giving complete help on No. 5 posting up.

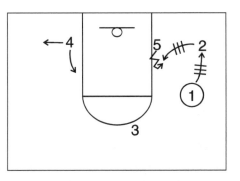

C

If No. 1 reverses the ball to No. 3, No. 4 looks to post up on the weak side. Player No. 5, in turn, steps out off of the lane and screens No. 2's defender. Player No. 2 sets his defender up with a fake and looks for a pass on the cut into the lane.

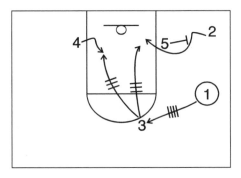

A

If you have an outstanding shooter, Diagrams A and B give the option of bringing the shooter (No. 3) back to the ball. Player No. 1 dribbles off of No. 4's screen. At the same time, No. 3 runs along the baseline receiving screens by No. 5 and No. 2.

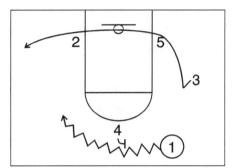

B

Player No. 1 reverses the ball to No. 4 who dribbles it to the wing as No. 5 posts up. As this is taking place, both No. 1 and No. 2 double screen for No. 3. This brings No. 3 back to the ball for a second chance of catching and scoring off of a curl cut.

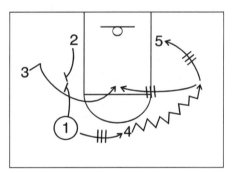

C

As an option out of this set, No. 1 dribbles off No. 4's screen as No. 3 runs the baseline. Player No. 1 passes the ball to No. 3.

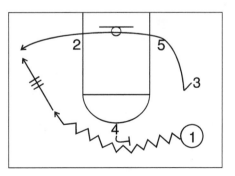

D

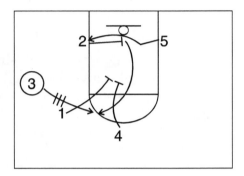

Once No. 3 has received the pass, No. 2 turns and screens away for No. 5 in the low post. Then both No. 1 and No. 4 double screen for No. 2 as No. 2 comes up the middle of the lane looking for the shot. This is a good "counter" if No. 3 has no shot.

E

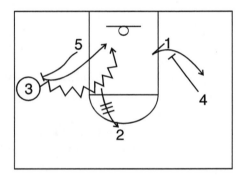

If No. 2 does not receive the pass and No. 3 doesn't post feed No. 5, No. 5 can step out on the wing and screen on the ball for a pick-and-roll.

High/Low
Post Sets

A

Player No. 1 dribbles toward the wing and passes to No. 3. Player No. 1 then cuts to the ballside wing. Player No. 4 steps out to screen for No. 3.

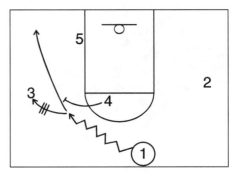

B

Player No. 4 screens on the ball as No. 3 looks for the opening to shoot, dribble or pass off of the screen. Player No. 2 stays wide and spots up for a pass. Player No. 5 backscreens for No. 1 as No. 3 dribbles off of No. 4's screen. After setting the screen, No. 4 has three options:

1) Pop back for a shot.
2) Pick-and-roll.
3) Screen for No. 5.

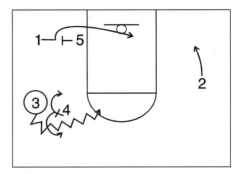

A

This is out of a high low set with a two guard front. Player No. 1 makes the guard-forward pass and cuts and replaces himself. Player No. 2 makes a cut off of the high post looking for a layup. Player No. 1 takes a return pass from No. 3.

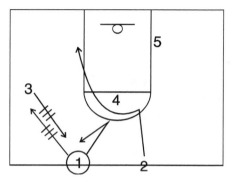

B

As soon as No. 2 has cut past No. 4 and No. 4 sees No. 2 has not received a pass, No. 4 rolls down the lane opposite the ball. Player No. 1 takes the ball toward the double screen. As soon as No. 2 makes his cut, No. 5 curls into the lane around No. 4 for a quick step in move. If No. 4's defender blocks No. 5, No. 4 steps up toward the ball. Player No. 2 will cut under the double either curling back into the lane or flaring to the corner.

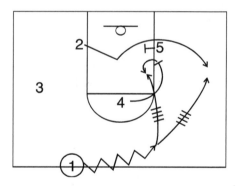

A

This is a high post set that relies on misdirection much like a play in football. As No. 4 screens for No. 1, both wings cross out. The intervention is to create a "pursuit" situation by No. 2 and No. 2's defenders in that they will chase No. 2 and No. 3 as they cross out.

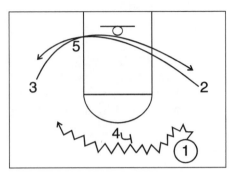

B

After No. 1 dribbles to the wing, he reverses the ball back to No. 4 who passes to No. 3. With the ball being taken to the wing by No. 1, it is assumed No. 2's defender will be in a denial position (even if No. 2 and No. 3's defenders switch) being one pass away. Once No. 3 has the ball, No. 5 backscreens for No. 2 along the baseline for a layup.

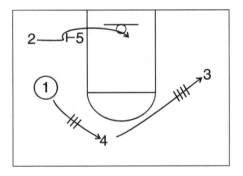

A

This is out of a high post 2-3 set. Player No. 1 passes to the wing and both guards "X" off of No. 5 who is positioned at the free-throw line. After both guards cut, No. 5 receives a pass from No. 3.

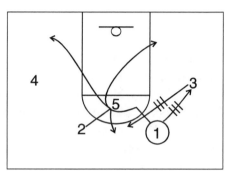

B

Player No. 5 reverses the ball to No. 4 and, after No. 4 catches the ball, No. 2 steps up to backscreen for No. 5. If the lob presents itself, the pass should be encouraged.

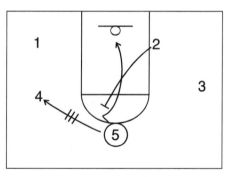

C

After No. 5 cuts to the basket, he looks to post in the middle of the lane. He positions himself this way because now his defender must decide how to guard him. Player No. 4 passes to No. 2 who looks right down the middle of the lane to No. 5.

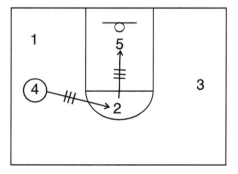

A

This action is out of a two guard front with the wings at the free-throw line extended. Player No. 1 passes to No. 3 who has stepped up to about the top of the circle to receive the pass. Both No. 1 and No. 2 receive flare screens from the wings. Player No. 3 looks for the open man for the jump shot.

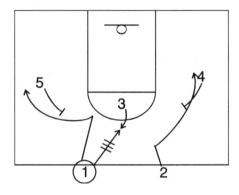

B

If the wings are not open, No. 3 can pass to either No. 4 or No. 5. Here No. 4 receives the pass.

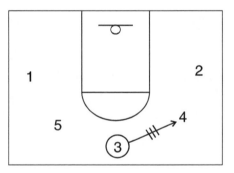

C

Player No. 2 can go backdoor for a layup if he is overplayed as No. 3 and No. 5 set staggered screens for No. 1. Player No. 1 then comes off of the screens looking for a jump shot or curl move into the lane for a layup.

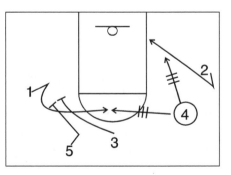

A

This play is designed to isolate an outside shooter and a post-up player on one side of the floor. Player No. 1 passes to No. 2 and cuts off of the high post. Both No. 5 and No. 3 are stacked on the opposite block.

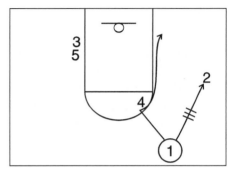

B

Player No. 2 passes to No. 4 who turns with the basketball and faces the basket. Player No. 4's first look is to the weak side as No. 3 steps his defender into the lane as No. 5 turns and screens for him.

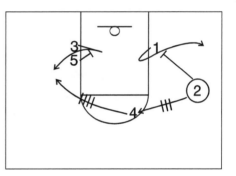

A

This is a variation of the UCLA High Post Offense. Player No. 1 passes to the wing and cuts off the high post looking for a return pass. Player No. 1 empties out opposite as No. 4 dives to the opposite block.

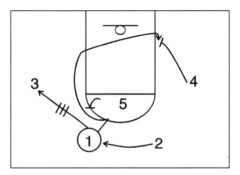

B

Player No. 3 reverses the ball to No. 2 and cuts to set a double screen for No. 1 (who has stacked behind No. 5).

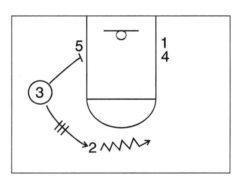

C

Player No. 1 now has the option of curling on No. 4's side or cutting across the lane under No. 3 and No. 5's double stack set.

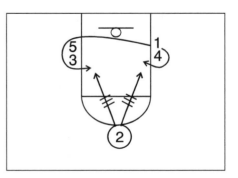

A

This is an option out of the UCLA high post offense. Player No. 1 hits No. 3 and then cuts off of No. 5. Player No. 2 and No. 4 are stacked on the weak side. If No. 1 is open for a layup, No. 3 passes to No. 1.

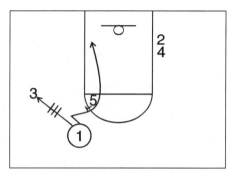

B

Player No. 3 receives the ball but doesn't hit No. 1 on his cut. Player No. 5 screens on the ball. Player No. 3 dribbles off of the screen looking for penetration. At the same time No. 5 continues down the lane to screen for No. 1, Player No. 4 screens for No. 2 on the weakside block. Player No. 2 looks to read the defense and will either curl or flare. No. 4 then steps toward the ball if X4 helps on No. 2's cut.

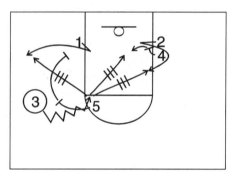

A

Player No. 1 passes to No. 2 as No. 5 comes up to set a flare screen to free No. 1 on the wing. Player No. 2 passes to No. 4 and cuts into the lane to screen for No. 5. Player No. 4 can pass to No. 5 directly. This initial alignment affords the offense the quick opportunity for the jump shot by No. 1 and it also gives a big man (No. 5) a drive to the hoop for the high/low pass.

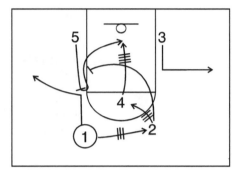

B

If No. 4 passes to No. 3, No. 5 posts up to catch. Player No. 2 cuts underneath No. 5 for a possible shot or post feed from the baseline. Player No. 1 backscreens for No. 4 for a lob.

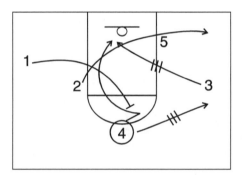

C

The ball is reversed from No. 3 to No. 1 to No. 4. Player No. 2 sets his man up and makes a curl cut into the lane looking for a layup.

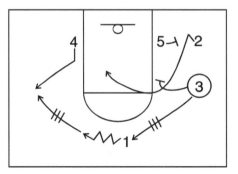

A

This is a quick hitter and a rather safe play in that it does not start with a pass. The use of the dribble entry gives the defense the opportunity to set itself on the ballside wing. The attack then comes from the blind side of the defense. Player No. 1 dribbles to the wing as No. 3 cuts to the block to post up. Player No. 2 at the same time cuts underneath No. 3 on the ball side. As soon as No. 2 cuts past No. 4, No. 4 backscreens No. 5 for a lob pass.

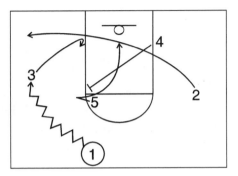

A

Player No. 3 pops out of the high post to the wing then stacks with No. 5. Player No. 4 flashes to the high post. Player No. 1 passes to No. 4 and No. 2 cuts backdoor immediately (No. 2 may be open for a layup right away if he can beat his defender). If not, No. 2 continues underneath the double screen for a possible jump shot.

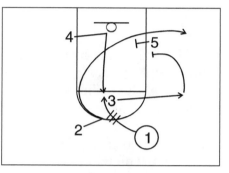

B

Option: Player No. 3 remains on the wing instead of stacking up with No. 5. Player No. 2 cuts backdoor but pops back onto the wing. Player No. 5 steps up to the screen for No. 3 for a shuffle cut into the lane.

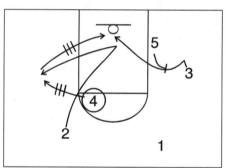

C

Player No. 4 can pass to No. 2 and dive to the ballside block for a post up situation.

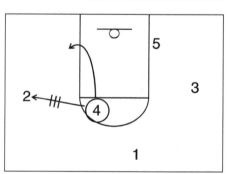

D

Player No. 3 then flashes into the high post. When No. 3 catches, he looks low to No. 4. From this triangle alignment many options are available.

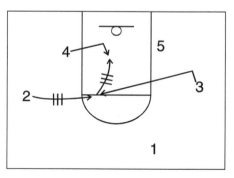

E

If No. 2 has the basketball, No. 4 can screen across the lane for No. 5 and then No. 3 screens for No. 4 (pick-the-picker).

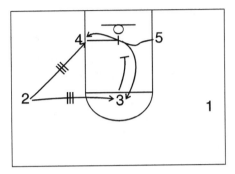

F

Player No. 4 can remain on the ballside block posting up from the ball as No. 3 screens away for No. 5 at the opposite block.

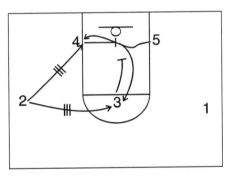

G

Player No. 5 can backscreen for No. 3.

H

Player No. 3 and No. 4 can set a double screen for No. 5.

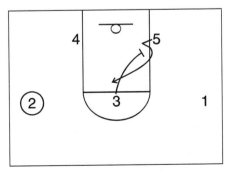

I

In a continuation from the original set (Diagram A), No. 2 enters the ball to the left wing and No. 1 cuts to the ballside corner.

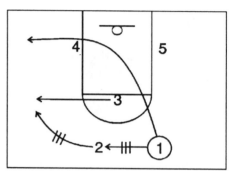

J

As No. 1 is cutting through the lane, No. 5 is moving up to backscreen No. 2's man for a lob pass from No. 3.

A

Player No. 1 passes to No. 4 and both guards cut through the lane. This is a 2-3 set in which the guards "X" off of the high post. The intention is to isolate No. 5 and No. 3 in the lane for a two-man game.

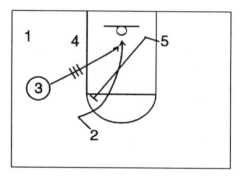

B

Player No. 5 then turns and screens for No. 3. If the defense switches, No. 5 rolls back to the ball to the basket.

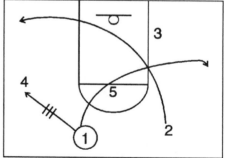

Quick
Hitters

A

This is a quick hitter that can be used in either a half-court set or out of a secondary break. Player No. 1 passes to No. 2 as No. 3 and No. 5 double screen for a flair and skip pass back to No. 1.

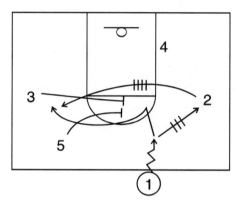

A

This set has a number of quick-hit options. Player No. 1 brings the ball to No. 3's side. Player No. 3 can cut backdoor for a layup if he is overplayed. If the backdoor does not present itself, No. 1 reverses the ball to No. 4 who, in turn, looks inside. Player No. 2, who stacks underneath No. 5, must read the defense. Player No. 2 can flair to the wing for a jump shot or post feed, or No. 2 can curl cut around No. 5. Player No. 2 looks for a layup here. After No. 2 makes the curl, No. 5 steps right behind No. 2 into the lane as No. 5 will help on No. 2's curl.

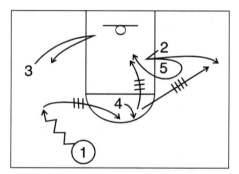

A

The play begins with No. 5 screening down for No. 3. Player No. 1 passes to No. 3 and then No. 1 screens away for No. 2.

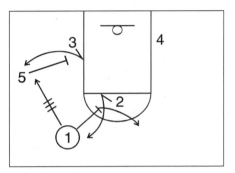

B

Player No. 3 passes to No. 2 and No. 4 flashes toward the ball looking for a possible pass. Player No. 3 then shuffle cuts off of No. 5's backscreen as No. 2 reverses the ball to No. 1 who looks for No. 3 for a possible layup.

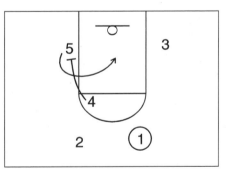

C

Player No. 4 then screens for No. 5 who curls into the lane for a short jump shot. (If No. 3 does not receive the pass for No. 1, he continues to the corner.)

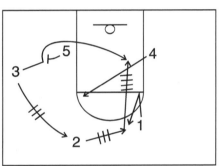

D

If neither 3 or 5 is open, the passing game begins.

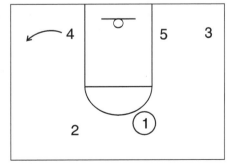

A

This is a good quick hitter for either a 3-point attempt or for an isolation for No. 5. Players No. 2, 3 and 4 line up along the free-throw line. Player No. 1 takes the ball to the wing looking to post feed No. 5. Players 3 and 4 both screen for No. 2 who pops out for a quick jump shot. If one of the defenders switches, that offensive player goes into the lane.

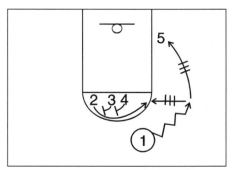

A

This is a simple cross screen at the free-throw line, but its goal is to create a mismatch with a post player attempting to guard a perimeter player. Player No. 1 takes the ball to the wing. Player No. 5 screens for No. 2 for a possible quick jump shot. Player No. 3 pops to the corner and No. 4 flexes across the lane. If No. 4 is fronted, throw the ball over the defender's head.

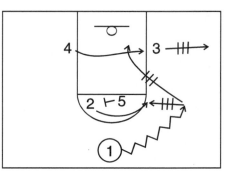

A

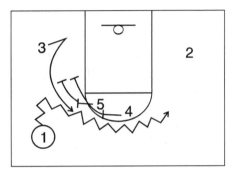

This is a quick hitter that can be run either out of a secondary break or in a half-court offense out of a box set with No. 4 and No. 5 starting at both elbows, and No. 2 and No. 3 at each block. Player No. 1 dribbles off a double staggered screen set by both No. 4 and No. 5. As No. 1 dribbles toward No. 2, No. 2 drifts toward the baseline spotting up for the jump shot. Players 4 and 5 continue to the other wing, setting another double screen for No. 3.

B

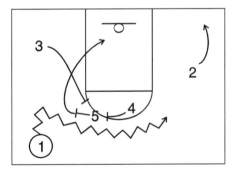

This is a variation of the previous play. No. 1 receives double staggered screens from No. 4 and No. 5. As No. 1 dribbles off the screens, No. 3 sets a backscreen for No. 5 who looks for a lob pass from No. 1.

A

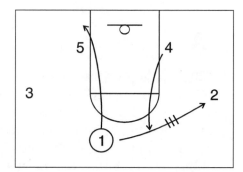

Pass to wing and point guard cuts to opposite block. Ballside postman comes high for a pass from No. 2. Player No. 1 will momentarily be stacked with No. 5. Player No. 1 will now read the defense as to which side of the floor he will use to receive the ball.

B

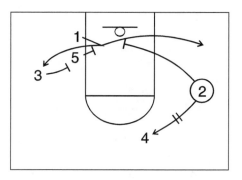

Players No. 1 and No. 2 will now cross out in the lane with No. 2 screening for No. 1. Again, No. 1 has the option of going either way. That is, accepting No. 2's single screen or taking the double screen on the weakside set by No. 3 and No. 5. If No. 1 accepts No. 2's screen, then No. 2 goes out opposite using screens from No. 5 and No. 3.

A

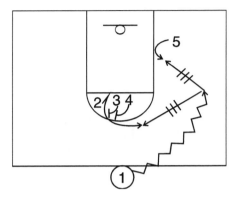

This play is designed to isolate the post player on the block while also creating an opportunity for a 3-point attempt. Player No. 1 takes the ball to the wing as No. 5 positions himself for a post feed. While this is occurring, both No. 3 and No. 4 turn to screen for No. 2.

A

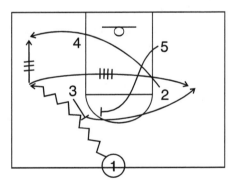

This set is designed for either a post-up or for a skip pass and 3-point attempt. Player No. 3 steps up to screen for No. 1 as No. 1 takes the ball to the wing. At the same time, No. 2 cuts diagonally across the lane underneath No. 4. Player No. 5 back-screens No. 3 for a possible skip pass from No. 1 if No. 3's defender helps too much on the screen.

A

This play comes out of a high/low set with a two guard front. Player No. 1 passes to No. 3 and cuts off of the high post. As the ball is being passed to No. 3, No. 4 flashes across the lane to the ball side. If No. 1 is open for the lob, throw it!

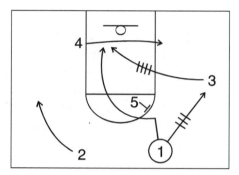

B

After No. 5 has screened for No. 1 and he sees the lob option is not available, No. 5 curls down the lane to set a double screen for No. 1 who uses the double screen on the baseline.

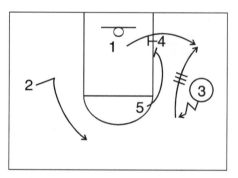

C

If you find that No. 5 is being over-played by his defender, have No. 1 fake the cut off of No. 5 after No. 3 has received the ball. Player No. 5 will then roll to the basket from the high post.

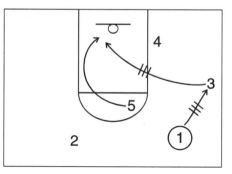

A

This is an excellent "end-of-the-game" play. It is out of a 3-2 set. Player No. 1 passes the ball to No. 2. Player No. 4 comes up to screen for No. 1 who cuts wide to the wing. Players 3 and 5 stay wide of the lane.

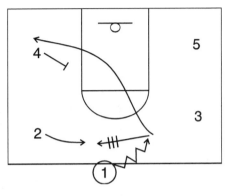

B

After No. 1 has gotten to the wing, No. 2 dribbles off of No. 4's screen. As No. 1 sees No. 2 bringing the ball toward him, No. 1 empties out through the lane to screen for No. 5. This screen is intended to create a mismatch and a layup for No. 5.

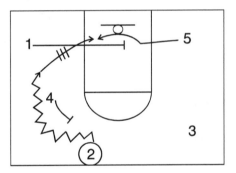

A

Player No. 5 screens on the ball as both No. 2 and No. 4 are set up on the free-throw line. As No. 1 comes off of No. 5's screen, No. 4 screens for No. 2. Player No. 2 must read his defender. If No. 2's defender follows over No. 4's screen, No. 2 curls around to the basket. If No. 2's defender goes underneath No. 4's screen, No. 2 flares to the wing for a quick pass and the shot. After No. 5 screens for No. 1, he continues on to screen for No. 3. Player No. 3 is looking for the jump shot at the top of the circle or he reads the defense for a possible backdoor cut.

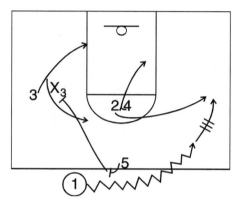

A

Player No. 3 crosses out and receives a staggered double screen from No. 4 and No. 2. Player No. 3 receives the pass from No. 1 and No. 1 cuts opposite to stack with No. 5.

B

Player No. 3 is momentarily isolated on the wing for a 1-on-1 move. Player No. 4 then comes up to screen on the ball. As No. 3 and No. 4 are executing a pick-and-roll or pick-and-pop (where No. 4 pops back for a jump shot), No. 2 goes underneath the stack set of No. 5 and No. 1.

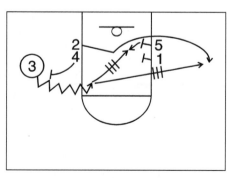

A

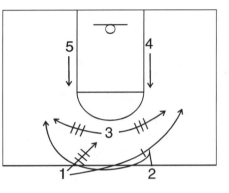

This is a quick hitter designed to create spacing for either a spot shot or for penetration. Player No. 1 passes to No. 3 who has spotted up above the top of the circle. Player No. 1 then screens across for No. 2. Both the screener, (No. 1) and the player screened for (No. 2) look for a pass for a 3-point shot. Players No. 4 and No. 5 come up the lane ready to screen.

B

If No. 1 and No. 2 can't get open after they cross, the two post players step out to screen for them. Players No. 1 and No. 2 can flare screen, curl or screen/rescreen in order to free themselves for a shot.

A

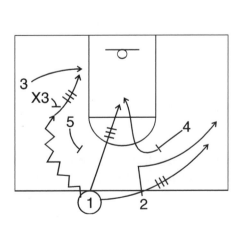

Another alignment that is ideal for a quick hitter is shown here with both big men above the free-throw line looking to screen. Player No. 1 can dribble off of No. 5's screen creating a potential help situation by No. 3's defender. This invites the backdoor cut by No. 3 for a layup. Player No. 4 screens for No. 2 leading to a skip pass and a jump shot by No. 2. Or, if No. 4's defender helps or No. 2's cut, No. 4 dives to the basket looking for a pass from No. 1.

A

This is a good set if you need a quick three point attempt or if you want to ensure that the best shooter will receive the ball. This quick hitter comes out of a single low post set as No. 1 passes to No. 4 on the wing and then cuts through. Player No. 2 rotates to fill No. 1's vacated spot and receives a return pass from No. 4.

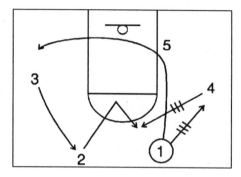

B

Player No. 2 passes to No. 3 as both No. 4 and No. 5 set up a double screen for No. 2 on the wing. Player No. 3 throws a skip pass to No. 2 for a jump shot.

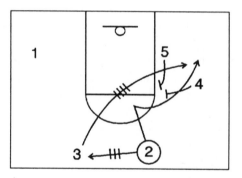

C

Option: If No. 2's defender slips through the double screen, No. 4 and No. 5 turn and rescreen No. 2's defender.

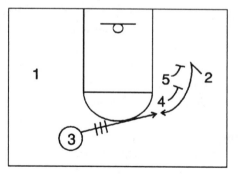